T0251092

Designing the User Experience of Game Development Tools

Designing
the User
Experience
of Game
Development
Tools

DAVID LIGHTBOWN

CRC Press
Taylor & Francis Group
Boca Raton London New York

CRC Press is an imprint of the
Taylor & Francis Group, an **informa** business

AN A K PETERS BOOK

CRC Press
Taylor & Francis Group
6000 Broken Sound Parkway NW, Suite 300
Boca Raton, FL 33487-2742

First issued in hardback 2017

Version Date: 20140919

ISBN-13: 978-1-4822-4019-1 (pbk)
ISBN-13: 978-1-138-42763-1 (hbk)

Library of Congress Cataloging-in-Publication Data

Lightbown, David.
  Designing the user experience of game development tools / David Lightbown.
      pages cm
  Includes bibliographical references and index.
    ISBN 978-1-4822-4019-1 (alk. paper)
    1. Computer games--Design. 2. Computer games--Evaluation. 3. Computer games--Psychological aspects. 4. Human-computer interaction. I. Title.

  QA76.76.C672L54 2015
  794.8'1536--dc23   2014034087

Visit the Taylor & Francis Web site at
http://www.taylorandfrancis.com

and the CRC Press Web site at
http://www.crcpress.com

Dedication

When I was young, I tried to convince my parents to buy a video game console. Instead, they bought a computer.

As a result, I played video games at my friends' houses and in arcades. On days when I wanted to play games at home, my only option was to try re-creating the games on our computer. To my surprise, I found that I enjoyed creating games as much as I did playing them. If my parents had bought a console, I might never have discovered my passion for game development.

My parents sacrificed their time and energy (and at times, their sanity) to teach me focus, patience, and the rewards that come from challenging yourself. Oh, the fact that they sent me to a great school didn't hurt either.

They provided me with the tools—intellectual as well as electronic—so that I could have one of the greatest gifts anyone could ever ask for: a job that I look forward to every day, where I have the privilege of making tools to help people turn their ideas into reality.

Thanks, Mom and Dad. I love you!

Contents

Praise for *Designing the User Experience of Game Development Tools*

"As a technical artist, I've been espousing the benefits of tools for artists and production pipelines for more than a decade. But honestly, they've been bare-bones, just-get-the-job-done kind of quality. It's about time we attach some professionalism to the design of our tools as well. User experience is the preeminent design challenge of our time and David has captured and refined these concepts to help us produce beautifully designed workflows that are a pleasure to use. His acclaimed lectures, now demonstrated and elaborated in this book, are brilliant and very appropriate to our industry. My toolsets going forward are going to incorporate as many of these concepts as I can squeeze into them."

—Jason Parks
Owner, Continuity AI (former Technical Artist for SCEA, THQ, and Volition)

"Lightbown tackles some complicated cognitive and scientific concepts, but does so in a completely conversational manner that is not only approachable, but fun and interesting to read. His examples are worth sharing, and putting them into action has definitely made me a better designer."

—Jim Brown
Epic Games

"David Lightbown's book shines a light on a dark corner of the games, but it's a corner on the path we take every day in game development. All developers owe it to their future selves to learn to apply the process presented in this book to their tools."

—Corey Johnson
Unity Technologies

"If you build games tools and are not familiar with User-Centered Design, then you should read this book. David explains why the user experience of the tools you make is important to your users and how it has a positive impact on your bottom line. He provides a comprehensive introduction to User-Centered Design with easy-to-understand explanations and plenty of real-world examples that demonstrate the principles and best practices you need to know to start building better tools today."

—Tom Hoferek
Principal User Experience Designer, Autodesk

"Through honest insight and real-world pragmatism, David has provided a wonderful entry point to the practice of User-Centered Design while highlighting its practical application to game development tools. David not only delivers the concepts and techniques that can be used to improve the user experience of game development tools, he also outlines—in clear and measurable terms—the return on investment for doing so. A must read for anyone who's serious about improving the efficiency, creativity, and productivity of the content creators on their team."

—Liam Grieg
Senior UX Designer, Atlassian

"All too often, in-house software tools are neglected children, with baffling interfaces and steep learning curves, which translates into countless hours of lost productivity. In this easy-to-read, comprehensive guide, David Lightbown applies classic principles of User-Centered Design to the tool-building process, so that developers can help users unlock the power of their applications, and help stakeholders manage and measure their success. A must-read, even if you're not in the games industry."

—AJ Kandy
Co-Founder/Director of Design, Peterson/Kandy

Foreword

David and I first met just after the Game Developers Conference in 2012. The interface designer on my team had just given a presentation on our experience and approach to usability for our internal development tools. I think what sparked that first conversation was David's initial surprise that there was someone else, anyone else, out there in our space that really did care about these issues. Game development, especially in the console space that I'm most familiar with, is often very player-focused. We want to do what makes for the best player experience. As an industry and a culture we have a very long, fruitful history in that area. Much more rarely do we take that same expertise and focus it inward. How do we take the lessons of games and apply them to making games?

Over the last ten years or so, there has though been a growing realization among developers, especially on larger teams, that the cost and complexity of making games is itself inhibiting our collective ability to develop the best experience for the player. In just the previous generation of AAA game development it was quite clear to everyone that these secondary knock-on effects were actually not just significant, but possibly the most significant predictor of quality. The phrase "iteration time" was heard everywhere. We had collectively realized that in making games, like most creative endeavors, you get it wrong the first time. And the second time. And the third. But you learn something important in each iteration and the more iterations you can do, the better at it you become. This is no surprise to anyone on an individual scale. The real change was that no one could escape this universal truth any longer. Brute force works well to a point and that point has passed.

Many different "solutions" to that problem have appeared since then. In particular, it's hard not to recognize the introduction of Agile methodologies in particular into the game industry as a process response to this very problem—as much as its adherents will insist it's not a process.

While these methods from other industries brought along with them a lot of baggage of dubious value, they did help to crystalize one important idea into development culture: you cannot know everything in advance. This is not to say you cannot know anything in advance, which in my experience is clearly what some Agile adherents have chosen to believe—and is clearly stupid. But the very idea that you cannot plan for everything in a creative project, not just that you should not, was both compelling and self-evident in retrospect. We had never been able to plan everything. We just pretended we could.

Then in the last five years or so, everywhere things were happening at about the same time, which would help mature the concept of "iteration" into one of "usability." People were no longer asking whether they should iterate more but rather how to make those iterations more valuable. Usability as a discipline and usability research outside the game industry (as well as within the game industry, but still largely focused on the player experience) had helped to define what we meant by iteration. How does one improve or increase iterations not just by making long processes shorter, but by making things better or differently altogether? Where does a user and her expectations fit into all of this? The discipline of usability research was growing all around us to answer these kinds of questions. In particular, the meteoric rise of webapps and mobile development (games or otherwise) and the unprecedented success of the iPhone in particular brought usability design into the limelight. And then came Gamification: the much maligned, and in my view, both largely misunderstood and completely misapplied, idea that you could take the lessons learned from games and apply them to other things. Like making games.

It was as both David and I were preparing for GDC 2013 that I think we found where all of this would lead us. I was preparing my presentation "Usability Is Not Random" based on my theory that usability could be formalized in terms of information and information theory. We can describe our interactions with our tools as a form of communication, which we could measure and analyze. I could use this model to help improve and guide my approach to developing tools with my team, in my day job as engine director at Insomniac Games.

David, however, was driven by something even larger. That same year, we were both part of a Google Hangout panel together. We discussed what drove us and what was most important to us. It became clear that what David wanted was not just to figure out how much he could improve the usability of a specific tool or set of development tools or even for a specific team, but that he wanted to improve usability everywhere in our industry. David is guided by his belief that he can contribute to raising the bar for all of us: that we can all speak the same language, understand the same concepts, and use the same techniques, so that we can all make better games.

What you are reading now is the result of David Lightbown's first big mission on that very long quest. The rest is a co-op campaign, and he has brought along these weapons to get us started.

Mike Acton
Engine Director
Insomniac Games
June 20, 2014

Introduction

Even though they had been trying for over an hour, the two men could not get the machine to perform its greatest trick: print a double-sided page. They were almost ready to give up. "We're S.O.L.," one of them said, finally. Fortunately, the interaction analyst was watching, and she got it all on videotape.

THE BIG GREEN BUTTON

In 1983, Xerox introduced their most technologically advanced photocopier, the Xerox 8200. It had many innovative features for the time: double-sided printing and automatically collating pages, to name a few. However, customer service representatives started reporting that customers complained the machine was "too complicated." Ironically, Xerox advertised the machine as being simple to use—"All you have to do is push the green button."

Xerox was also one of the first companies to hire social anthropologists and psychologists to help with product development. This is how—a few years before the Xerox 8200 was introduced—a doctoral student with a background in interaction analysis started working at Xerox. Her name was Lucy Suchman.

When the Xerox executives learned what customers were saying about the machine, Lucy was asked to help figure out why. She requested that one of the machines be installed at the Palo Alto Research Center so she could watch people using it.*

Two of the participants were specifically chosen by Lucy from the internal staff. She put them in front of the machine, in a room equipped with

---

* The Xerox Palo Alto Research Center, more commonly known as Xerox PARC, would play a huge role in driving the field of human–computer interaction forward. Michael A. Hiltzik's *Dealers of Lightning* offers a fantastic history of Xerox PARC, the people involved in its rise and fall, and all of the companies that they would go on to influence, including Adobe, Microsoft, Pixar, and Apple.

a microphone and a camera, and gave them a series of tasks to perform. One of these tasks was to test a major selling point of the machine: duplex print, or printing double-sided.

After an hour and a half of filling up the room with paper from failed attempts, the two men concluded that they could not figure it out. One of them expressed their frustration with a quote captured on the now-famous video recording: "We're S.O.L."

The video was presented to the Xerox executive as part of Lucy's report. After watching the video, one of the executives exclaimed that the reason the two men could not figure out how to print double-sided was that they are not smart enough. "You must have got these guys off the loading dock!"

That's when Lucy revealed that the two men she had chosen were actually two of the most gifted computer scientists working at Xerox: Ron Kaplan, a brilliant computational linguist, and Allen Newel, one of the founding fathers of artificial intelligence.

This was one of the first documented accounts of applying user research to improve an office productivity tool.* It would be many years before these techniques would be applied to tools development in the video games industry.

MY STORY

License to Compute

When I was a teenager, one of my first full-time jobs was working technical support for an Internet service provider. In the early days of the Internet, everyone who worked in technical support could do a bit of UNIX shell scripting and knew how to configure TCP/IP for every imaginable operating system.

All day long, we would answer calls from people who did not know as much about computers as we did, and we found it frustrating. To blow off steam, we would make fun of the customers when we got off the phone. One of the more infamous stories was that of a customer who was worried that they had "deleted the Internet," because they had accidentally dragged the Internet Explorer icon into the trash. After getting off a particularly difficult call, I remember saying to my colleagues that people should have to pass an exam to use a computer.

---

* The full version of this story can be found in Lucy Suchman's book *Human–Machine Reconfigurations.*

I realize now what a foolish statement that was. The problem is not the user. It is the user experience.

My Best and Worst Days in Game Development

Years later, I was fortunate enough to get my first job in the games industry. In that time, I have held a variety of roles, such as modeler, technical artist, and technical director.

Some of my best days working as a technical director were when I would watch how a change to a tool or pipeline could make an artist, animator, or level designer more productive. It always made me feel good when they would say, "That tool you worked on really saved me a lot of time, and I was able to focus on creating!" Nothing makes me happier than enabling content creators to do what they do best.

By contrast, some of my worst days were when I would walk by someone's desk and watch them jump through multiple frustrating and inefficient hoops, just to make a tiny bit of progress. Even if they didn't get much done, at least they could feel that they accomplished something. Seeing content creators limited in their ability to express themselves for reasons beyond their control is extremely frustrating to watch.

At that time, I had a limited set of options at my disposal, such as writing scripts to accelerate productivity, mentoring and coaching, trying to find ways to streamline the pipeline, and so on. However, I always felt that there was more that I could do to improve the tools. Without a doubt, my experience in the games industry gave me an advantage when it came to tools development, but no one can get it right every time. I needed to find a more consistent and measurable way.

This desire to help the content creators—whose work I admired so much—led me down a path that would change my career in the games industry.

Discovering the Inmates

One of my work colleagues at the time, who knew that I was looking for ways to make content creators more productive, handed me a copy of *The Inmates Are Running the Asylum*. This book—written by Alan Cooper, the creator of Visual Basic—had been circulating in web and desktop software development studios but had not yet made its way into game development. When I read it, I was amazed at how perfectly it captured the software development culture that I had been a part of across many different game development teams.

This book also introduced me to the field of user experience design. From the first day that I started working in game development, I had thoughts and opinions on how to design game development tools that would make the users more productive, but I was never able to pinpoint a system or methodology to do it consistently. This book opened the door to a world that I never even knew existed.

After finishing that book, I started to seek out any other books on user experience design that I could get my hands on: Don Norman's *The Design of Everyday Things*, Steve Krug's *Don't Make Me Think!*, Dan Saffer's *Designing for Interaction*, and Jeff Gothelf's *Lean UX*, to name just a few.

It wasn't long before I came to the realization that the concepts presented in these books had never been formally applied to tools development in the games industry. The untapped potential for improvement was huge.

The Main Message

I created a presentation about the impact that these concepts could have on tools development in the games industry, and I started showing it around to various game development studios. That presentation was essentially my job interview. This resulted in a full-time position focusing on improving the user experience of game development pipelines and tools at Ubisoft Montreal.

I would go on to give that presentation at least a dozen more times, most notably at the Montreal International Game Summit (MIGS) and the Game Developers Conference (GDC), where the feedback from the attendees put it among the most highly rated presentations of both conferences. A featured article on Gamasutra followed.

No long after, I was approached to turn the presentation into a book, which you now hold in your hands. The main message of the presentation and of this book remains the same: the games industry needs to make the user experience of tools a priority.

WHO SHOULD READ THIS BOOK?

This book is for anyone who makes, uses, or benefits from game development tools. However, anyone involved in the production of video games in general should be aware of the message in this book, because it is my belief that investing in better tools can help us make better games.

The People Who Make the Tools, or "Developers"

Some tools developers have a reputation for not caring about the user experience of game development tools. This is largely unfair: most tools developers want to improve the user experience but are not given the time, lack the techniques, or do not know where to begin. This books aims to address those issues and empower tools developers to make positive steps toward improving the user experience of their tools.

Technical directors and technical artists are often in one of the best positions to initiate change, since they act as a bridge between the users and the developers. Many of them are also tools developers in their own right. This book will give them the knowledge to make the most of that position and improve the process with which our tools are developed.

The People Who Use the Tools, or "Users"

The term *content creators* is sometimes used to describe anyone who uses the tools to create content that will appear in the game, though most people simply know them as "the users." This can include modelers, animators, level designers, game designers, audio engineers, special effects artists, and so on. This book can help them improve communication with those responsible for making the tools and assist in identifying common issues, as well as proposing how they can be improved.

The People Who Benefit from the Tools, or "Stakeholders"

The people who benefit from the content produced by the tools are sometimes called *stakeholders*. These people may never use or even see the tools we that discuss in this book. Despite this, they can be the most important players, since they—sometimes indirectly—mandate the creation of the tools. Creative directors, producers, and managers are a few examples of people who belong to this group. As they are responsible for setting the requirements for the game and providing the resources to create it, it is of the utmost importance that they understand that improving the user experience can reduce risk, as well as save time and money.

A Note for User Experience Designers

If you are a user experience designer coming from another industry, you will be familiar with many of the concepts in this book. You will notice that some concepts and techniques have been simplified in an effort to be easier to understand for people new to user experience design.

However, this book also includes a lot of information specific to game tools development. The games industry faces unique challenges in regard to improving the user experience of their tools. It is those challenges that make the work even more interesting for user experience designers: there is a lot of work to do but also a ton of untapped potential, waiting to be unlocked.

It Can Take Years to Become an Expert in User Experience

Although this book strives to be as thorough as possible at presenting ways in which the user experience can be improved, it cannot turn you into a user experience expert overnight. If your goal is to become an expert, it will take time and dedication—and by reading this book, you are taking your first big step.

For the Gamers

When I visit my local game store, I make a point of listening to people in the store talk about games. It reminds me that the content we create with our tools is ultimately for the gamers. Hearing people get excited about upcoming games and talking about their experiences can remind us why we love making games in the first place.

COMPANION WEBSITE AND TWITTER ACCOUNT

Although the content of this book is static, there are a few resources available to make it dynamic and interactive. The companion website, www.UXofGameTools.com, contains the latest information and revisions for this book, as well as contact information. You can also follow the official Twitter account @UXofGameTools to see the latest updates and read a curated list of articles related to user experience.

Your questions and comments are all welcome, so please feel free to contact me via e-mail at UXofGameTools@gmail.com or through the Twitter account.

BEFORE WE BEGIN …

The concepts and techniques in this book reflect my approach to improving the user experience of game development tools, and it is by no means the only way. Just as I have borrowed ideas on user experience design from other sources and tailored them to fit game tools development, you should take what works best for you and your situation.

In addition, this is not an academic text, so some concepts have been simplified for those who are learning about user experience for the first time. Wherever possible, I have added resources in the footnotes for people who want more details.

Some of the ideas in this book may be very new and different if you have been developing game tools for a long time. Keep in mind that the goal is not to completely change the way we work, but to enhance it. The material presented here is to complement our existing skills, in an effort to make us better game developers.

At the end of the day, as long as the users, stakeholders, and developers work together to make better tools, there is no right or wrong way.

Now, let's jump in!

About the Author

After spending most of his formative years in his parents' basement trying to clone 8-bit console games on an Apple IIgs, **David Lightbown** got a job in the games industry. Since then, he has dedicated the majority of his career to working on content creation tools and pipelines.

In addition to contributing to a variety of games as a technical director, David has delivered presentations at the Game Developers Conference, Montreal International Game Summit, and SIGGRAPH, in various cities within Canada, the United States, and Europe.

He has also collaborated with Autodesk to create product reviews, training manuals, tutorial videos, and masterclasses. In 2010, he received the Autodesk Master Award for his contributions to the 3D community. The award also included a sweet leather jacket.

David current holds the title of technical director at Ubisoft Montreal.

CHAPTER 1

Welcome to Designing the User Experience of Game Development Tools

WHAT WILL WE LEARN IN THIS CHAPTER?

- What is this book about?

- What is a user experience?

- What is the value of improving the user experience?

- What are the parallels between user experience and games development?

- How do people benefit from improving the user experience?

- What happens when the needs of one group are prioritized over another?

WHAT IS THIS BOOK ABOUT?

The goal of this book is to present concepts and techniques that can be used to improve the user experience of game development tools. This book focuses on User-Centered Design, a process that revolves around understanding people's goals, watching them work, learning the context in which they work, and understanding how they think. We will learn how each phase of the process can contribute to improving the user experience.

Finally, we will see how this process can be applied to a real-world game development tool.

Before we learn about how to improve the user experience, it would be reasonable to begin by describing the term *user experience*.

DEFINING USER EXPERIENCE

If you do a web search or read books about user experience design, you will notice that there are many different ways to describe what a user experience is. One popular description comes from Elizabeth Sanders, who suggests that tools need to be "useful, usable, and desirable."* How are these three objectives prioritized?

The User Experience Pyramid

You may have heard about Maslow's hierarchy of human needs, which is often depicted as a pyramid. Essentially, it states that physiological needs—such as food and shelter—must be fulfilled before more complex needs are met—such as creativity and confidence (see the left side of Figure 1.1).†

The same goes for the user experience. The basic needs and expectations of a person using a tool must be met before considering functionality that is more advanced. In this case, a tool should be useful before it can be usable, and a tool should be usable before making it desirable (see the right side of Figure 1.1).

In other words, a tool may have a nice-looking user interface (desirable), but if it is difficult to use (not usable) and does not fulfill the user's needs (not useful), it can result in a bad user experience.

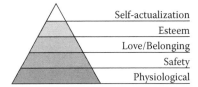 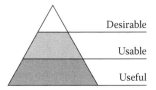

FIGURE 1.1   Maslow's hierarchy of human needs (left). The user experience pyramid (right).

---

* This was originally proposed in an article for the *Design Management Journal*, entitled "Converging Perspectives." It can be found here: http://onlinelibrary.wiley.com/doi/10.1111/j.1948-7169.1992. tb00604.x/abstract.
† You can read more about Maslow's hierarchy of human needs here: http://en.wikipedia. org/wiki/Maslow's_hierarchy_of_needs.

Unfortunately, some game development tools only provide the base level of the pyramid: they are useful. That also means that they are neither usable nor desirable. In the case of in-house tools, people use them because they have no other choice. To learn how we can make tools that people want to use, we can start by understanding the three levels.

Useful

At the core of a good user experience is something that fulfills a need. If a game development tool does not fulfill a need, why does it exist in the first place? Ideally, these needs should come from the users and the stakeholders.

To explain this further, we will use the analogy of a vehicle. As this is a book about game development tools, we will use a Warthog from the *Halo* franchise. A Warthog fulfills a Spartan's need to get from point A to point B in a short amount of time. It is faster—and in the case of enemy fire, often safer—than running. If we were to design a Warthog that simply fulfilled the need to get from point A to point B, it might resemble a frame with wheels, a turret, and an engine (see Figure 1.2).

How do we make a tool that is considered useful? We start by identifying the right people to design for and the context in which they work and by understanding their goals. We will talk more about this in Chapters 3 and 4.

This Warthog gets us from point A to point B, but it has a major issue: we are sitting on a metal platform with wheels. We have no protection, we are not comfortable, and it is not easy to use: the only way to drive is to reach our hands into the engine and connect the wires. There is no visible way to control the turret. Surely, there must be a better way! That brings us to the next level in the pyramid: making tools that are more usable.

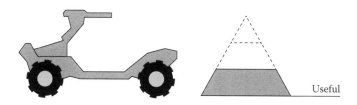

FIGURE 1.2   A user experience that is useful.

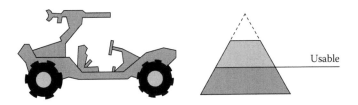

FIGURE 1.3   A user experience that is usable.

Usable

Much like user experience, there are many definitions of usability. The vast majority of these definitions include questions such as "How efficient is it to use?", "How easy is it to learn?", "How well is the user protected from making mistakes?", and "How satisfying is it to use?" There are many ways to measure improvements to usability, but in this book, we will focus on two: efficiency and learnability.

To continue with our example of the Warthog, what would be the definition of making it more usable? We could add pedals and a seat that is adjustable so the driver can sit comfortably and reach the pedals with their feet. This would make it convenient to accelerate and decelerate, without having to reach into the engine and connect any wires. To make it easier to learn how to drive and shoot the turret, we could add standard controls that any Spartan who has received basic training is familiar with: a pistol grip and a steering wheel (see Figure 1.3).

How do we improve usability? There are a variety of techniques, based on human factors, interaction design, cognitive psychology, and information architecture—just to name a few—that we will learn about in Chapter 5.

What else could be done to improve our Warthog? This question brings us to the third level of the pyramid: desirability. This is often dismissed as simply making the interface look "cool," but there is much more to it than that.

Desirable

Desirability is often the last step that we consider when designing game development tools. Typically, the perception is that desirability is not important or does not contribute enough to the user experience to make it worth the cost.

However, the fact is that a tool with an aesthetic and appealing design not only contributes to user satisfaction, but it also confirms to the user

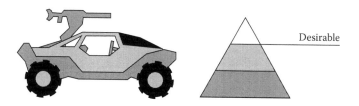

FIGURE 1.4   A user experience that is desirable.

that the designers have taken the time to create a high-quality, profes-sional tool. This gives the user more confidence in the abilities of the tool.

Let's return to our example of the Warthog. Features like tinted win-dows, shining chrome, and a new paint job may seem unnecessary, but consider this: if the windows are cracked, the labels on the controls are peeling off, and the body is covered in rust and falling apart, how confi-dent would you be that this Warthog will protect you in battle? You might ask yourself, "What else is wrong with the vehicle that I can't see? Is this going to keep me safe on the battlefield?" (see Figure 1.4).

Usability and desirability are often intertwined. We will see this when we learn about the design techniques of hierarchy in Chapter 5, or heuris-tics such as aesthetic and minimalist design in Chapter 6.

Missing Levels

Now, imagine if the Warthog was missing only the "usable" level of the pyramid. It has wheels, an engine, and an armored shell, but you have to crouch down inside and fiddle with the wires to control the engine and steer. Furthermore, you would be sitting on a metal plate instead of in a seat, without a seatbelt. It might look nice, but it would not be very safe or convenient (see the left side of Figure 1.5).

Alternatively, you could have a Warthog that is missing just the "useful" level: it has a nice seat with a seatbelt, a steering wheel, pedals, and an armored shell, but it has no engine or wheels. It may look great and have all of the controls you need on the inside, but it is not going to get you from point A to point B, which is why you wanted to use it in the first place (see the right side of Figure 1.5).

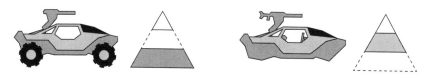

FIGURE 1.5   User experiences that are neither usable (left) nor useful (right).

Being "More Human"
Definitions from Cooper and Norman
Another common description of a good user experience is software that resembles an interaction with a human and not a machine.

In *The Inmates Are Running the Asylum*, Alan Cooper proposes that we should be "purposefully designing our software-based products to be more human and forgiving." An example of this would be a good friend, who would do the following:

- Remember what you like
- Do their best to help you
- Clearly explain themselves
- Take responsibility
- Be forgiving if something goes wrong
- Be flexible when trying to assist you

The artificial intelligence Cortana from the *Halo* series and the virtual assistant Siri from Apple are good examples of machines that appear to possess these qualities.

What is the opposite of that? A frustrating person. Don Norman echoes this in his book *The Design of Everyday Things* with examples on how to make something difficult to use on purpose: "Be inconsistent," "Be impolite." Everyone has had to deal with someone like this in their life at one point or another. A frustrating person does the following:

- Forgets what you like
- Will not help you
- Does not communicate clearly
- Does not take responsibility
- Is not forgiving if something goes wrong
- Is not flexible in helping you

The evil artificial intelligence SHODAN from *System Shock* would be an extreme example of this, or even GLaDOS from the game *Portal*.

How many tools can you think of that resemble a good friend? Now, how many can you think of that resemble a frustrating person?

Comparing the User Experience of Normal Mapping Tools
CrazyBump (Figure 1.6) is an excellent example of a content creation tool that feels "more human." It uses simple language that a human might use ("Intensity" and "Very Large Detail"). It communicates clearly by using previews to show you what will happen if you choose a specific option. It tries to help you by choosing the best option automatically. This makes the tool less intimidating and encourages users to make it part of their pipeline. Most importantly, it also means people are more likely to recommend it to their friends and coworkers.

Another example of this is the Unity engine: when you assign a texture that has characteristics of a normal map but you forget to flag it as such, the engine automatically detects this and offers to flag it as a normal map. This is a great example of software acting like a good friend by doing its best to help you (see the left side of Figure 1.7, at the bottom).

We can compare this to the NVIDIA Normal Map Filter on the right side of Figure 1.7. It resembles an interaction with a frustrating person. It is unclear what the options do, just like someone who does not communicate clearly, the 3D View forgets the last angle that you set it to after you close and reopen the window, and so on.

THE VALUE OF IMPROVING THE USER EXPERIENCE OF OUR TOOLS

In 2010, Jim Brown of Epic Games presented a talk at the Game Developers Conference titled "Tools: Making a Better Game." In this presentation, he stated that even a small increase in efficiency could result in a significant savings of time and money, when you look at the big picture. Some improvements may not seem like a lot on their own, but they can add up to hundreds of thousands of dollars and many man-months if you design it for the right people.

To illustrate this, let us assume that we take the time to improve the efficiency of a tool and make it easier to learn. Those improvements result in a savings of 20 minutes per 8-hour day. This may not seem like a lot on its own. However, we have to consider how many people are using that tool, and how often. If that tool is used by 20 users per 8-hour day, 20 minutes per day can save the following:

- 7 hours per day
- 32 hours per week
- 1,800 hours per year

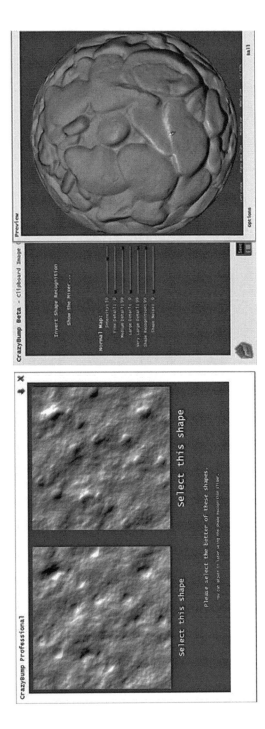

FIGURE 1.6   The CrazyBump interface. © Ryan Clark.

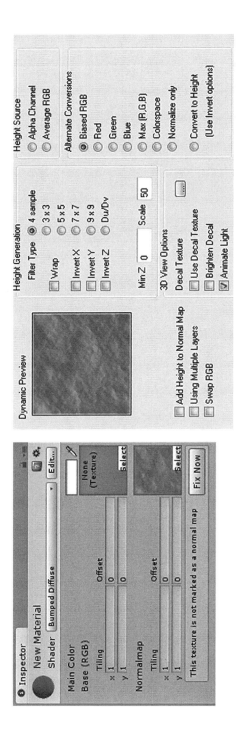

FIGURE 1.7   The Unity Inspector does its best to help you by making it easy to convert a material to a normal map (left). The NVIDIA Normal Map Filter has an overwhelming number of options that are not communicated clearly (right).

Now, when budgeting the staff for a game development team, you also have to consider salary, floor space, equipment, software, and many other details. As of this writing, the typical cost per man-month on the East Coast of North America is about $10,000. This means that if we save 20 users 20 minutes per day, after a year we can save the following:

- 100 man-months

- $100,000

If we invest $40,000 to make these changes, the return on investment is $60,000. In the second year, if the improvements are still saving us 20 minutes per day, we get a full $100,000. Over three years, if 20 users are still saving 20 minutes per 8-hour day, the total return on investment is $260,000. All for an initial $40,000 investment.

There will always be a difference between these predictions and the actual results. However, even if the real numbers are half of what we predicted, we still come out ahead in the end. The bottom line is that investing in the user experience of our tools has the potential to save us time and money.

PARALLELS BETWEEN USER EXPERIENCE AND GAME DESIGN

Some people may be surprised to learn that there are many similarities between the techniques used to make games and those used in user experience design. We are very fortunate that this is the case, because it can make the adoption of these techniques for game development tools less intimidating compared to other industries, such as banking, sales, or manufacturing.

Personas and Characters

In Chapter 4, you will learn about personas: profiles of people that represent the average user. In situations where there are a large number of users for a given tool, these can be very useful for making design decisions and giving everyone a shared vision of who will use the tools.

Though some people find the concept of using archetypes of people to help us make design decisions strange, think about this: we create characters in our games and consider how they think and what their goals are when writing their dialogue, creating the environments they live in, and so on. This has worked well for the creation of our games, so why not our tools?

Scenario Storyboards and Cinematic Storyboards

When creating game development tools, we often fixate on features without knowing how and when those features will be used. Scenario storyboards help to remind us of the context in which a tool is used. This can be an extremely important and powerful concept in user experience design. We will learn more about this in Chapter 4.

While it may seem odd to some people that we would create something like this for game development tools, keep in mind that we use storyboards for cinematics and complex gameplay moments too. We use them to plan and estimate risk, as opposed to going straight into implementing everything at full quality, which can be expensive and risky. There is no reason our tools cannot benefit from this technique as well.

Pre-Visualization and Gameplay Videos

Pre-visualizations, which we will learn more about in Chapter 6, come in all shapes and sizes with various levels of quality: sketches, paper prototypes, interactive prototypes, and so on. Regardless of the form, the goal is the same: simulate the user experience so we can get feedback from the user early, to ensure we are going in the right direction. All too often, the first time the user has a sense of how a tool works is when it is already done, and that is often one of the main reasons why a tool can have a bad user experience.

By comparison, gameplay videos have a similar goal: creating a video that simulates what the gameplay looks like in an effort to get feedback early. It may even be semi-interactive: there can be several small videos used as "branch-points" to show the outcome of different situations. As with pre-visualization, the visual fidelity of this video can vary, but the purpose remains the same: find out if we are going in the right direction. If we do this for our gameplay, why would we not apply the same concept to our tools?

Analytics and Metrics

Analytics may be more familiar to web and mobile app developers, but they can benefit game tools developers as well. Capturing statistics—such as who is using certain features, when they use them, and how often—can be an incredibly powerful technique for improving the user experience of your tool.

As we will discuss in Chapter 4, analytics are useful when you have a very large number of users and need help determining where to start. However, the results of analytics should not be the only source of information used to make design decisions. They should be used as a starting point before meeting your users face-to-face. Nothing helps you to understand how people use the tools like watching them work.

When a game is not running at the desired frame-rate, game developers capture metrics for the processor, graphics, and memory and then analyze them to identify what needs to be optimized. If you have done this before, you may be familiar with the tools provided by Microsoft and Sony, or the profiler tools in Unity, just to name a few. As with analytics, metrics can be a starting point as well. If a specific effect is causing the frame-rate to slow down, it does not necessarily mean that we cut it immediately. We prioritize based on how slow it is, take a closer look at why, and then see how it can be optimized.

If this technique is useful for figuring out what to optimize, we can certainly benefit from analytics to help us improve the user experience of our tools.

HOW DO PEOPLE BENEFIT FROM AN IMPROVED USER EXPERIENCE?

Users

If 20 users save 100 man-months, that theoretically translates to an extra five months per person. Think about how much more polish one person could do in five months. In addition, saving time can help with something else that is all too common in game development: overtime. It would be great if saving time resulted in users being able to work five days a week and go home before 6:00 to have time to themselves, or to see their family, while still being able to deliver a game with a high level of quality.

Stakeholders

For the people who mandate the tools, improving the user experience to save time and money is a business decision. If we can create content for our games more efficiently, and ramp up new team members faster, then we can allocate resources more effectively to make a better game.

In addition, the process presented in this book can give everyone a better vision of who is using the tools, and what is going to be built before we build it. This helps to reduce risk, giving stakeholders the ability to make better decisions.

Developers

For developers, there are multiple benefits. One of the most important benefits is not so much about improving the user experience, but the tools development process itself. In this book, we will learn about understanding what the users need, applying guidelines, and getting a clearer picture of what the tool will be before writing a single line of code. All of these concepts and techniques help to streamline the tools development process.

Finally, tools that work well survive the test of time. If a tool is inefficient or difficult to learn, people will want to replace it at the first opportunity. A good user experience will help to ensure that the tools we have worked so hard to create are used to make great games for years to come.

FINDING THE RIGHT BALANCE

As we discussed in the introduction, tools are mandated, created, and used by different groups of people who all have various needs. However, what happens when the needs of one group are prioritized over the needs of the others?

If the needs of the developers are prioritized, the tool could lose focus on achieving the goals of the business (important to the stakeholders) and could be difficult to use for creating game content (important to the users).

If the needs of the users are prioritized, the limitations of the technology may not be respected (important to the developers) and resources could be spent on features that are not important to creating the main content for the game (important to the stakeholders).

If the needs of the stakeholders are prioritized, the time to create a software architecture that is easy to maintain could be limited (important to the developers) and the tool could be unstable and frustrating to use (important to the users).

For a tool to be truly successful, the needs of developers, stakeholders, and users must all be equally balanced (see the extreme right side of Figure 1.8). One of the best ways to do this is by applying the User-Centered Design process, which is covered in the next chapter.

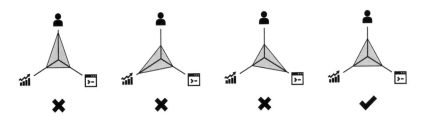

FIGURE 1.8 Finding the right balance between the needs of the users, stakeholders, and developers.

WRAPPING UP

In this chapter, we reviewed a few common definitions of "user experience," and we learned the value of improving the user experience. We also learned about the parallels between user experience design and game development, and we discussed how different groups of people can benefit from improving the user experience, as well as what happens when the needs of one of those groups is prioritized over another.

In the next chapter, we will learn about the User-Centered Design process, which is at the heart of improving the user experience of game development tools.

CHAPTER 2

The User-Centered Design Process

WHAT WILL WE LEARN IN THIS CHAPTER?

- What is the User-Centered Design process?

- How can User-Centered Design help us to achieve a better user experience faster?

- How can pre-visualization be used to improve the user experience?

- How can we integrate the User-Centered Design process into Agile (Scrum)?

- How do we deal with a lack of time to implement the User-Centered Design process?

WHAT IS THE USER-CENTERED DESIGN PROCESS?

The User-Centered Design process is one of the most widely used approaches to user experience design. It has been applied in a variety of different industries for many years. The majority of this book is focused on guiding you through each step in the process and, along the way, presenting concepts and techniques that can be used to improve the user experience of game development tools.

The most important concept to understand about the User-Centered Design process is that it is not a magic solution. There is no "secret sauce" that will provide immediate results, and it is not a "shiny coat of paint"

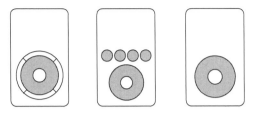

FIGURE 2.1   Iterative improvements to the iPod Classic scroll-wheel across several generations.

that can be applied at the end of development. It is an iterative process. Comparing the first few generations of the scroll-wheel on the Apple iPod (see Figure 2.1) reminds us that even very popular products take time and sometimes several iterations to get it right … and even then, they can always be improved.

By applying the User-Centered Design process, we accept that we may not get it right the first time. However, with each quick iteration, we will analyze the tool to find problems, make improvements to the design, and evaluate it with the users to confirm that we are going in the right direction.

THE PHASES OF THE USER-CENTERED DESIGN PROCESS

"It is a shift in attitude from designing *for users* to one of designing *with users*."

ELIZABETH SANDERS (EMPHASIS ADDED)

User-Centered Design is an iterative process that revolves around the users. Therefore, it should come as no surprise that the users are at the center of the process (see Figure 2.2). Everything that we do is done out of consideration for the users.

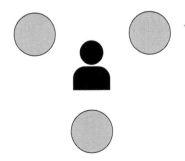

FIGURE 2.2   Each phase of the User-Centered Design process revolves around the users.

There are many different versions of this process used in user experience design, such as the ISO 9241-210 ISO standard for human–computer interaction.* We will use a simple and straightforward process for the purposes of this book, made up of the following phases: Analysis, Design, and Evaluation.

Analysis

This phase, which is covered in Chapter 4, is all about examining how people use the tools. We will learn the importance of watching users work, as opposed to relying only on focus groups, surveys, or simply asking the users to tell us how they think that they work. We will also learn how the brain processes actions and mental loads, which will help us find ways to make the tools better for the users.

Through a variety of techniques, we will learn how to observe and interpret the way in which people use the tools. We are not looking for solutions at this time; we are only focusing on identifying problems (see Figure 2.3).

Design

There is an old saying in the field of user experience: "Design without constraints is just art." One of the most important outputs of the Analysis phase is to provide us with those constraints, so that we can use them to choose what to improve during the Design phase. In this phase, beginning in Chapter 5, we will learn a number of concepts and techniques that we can use to improve the design (see Figure 2.4).

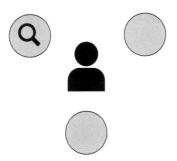

FIGURE 2.3   The Analysis phase of the User-Centered Design process.

---

* For more on the ISO 9241-210 standard, visit the website http://www.iso.org/iso/catalogue_detail. htm?csnumber=52075.

FIGURE 2.4   The Design phase of the User-Centered Design process.

Evaluation

Finally, we can move on to the Evaluation phase, which is covered in Chapter 6. Here, we will learn what a heuristic evaluation is. We will also learn how to build a test plan, which will allow us to determine if the changes to the design are improving the user experience. We will also determine when it is appropriate to go straight to code or to use pre-visualization techniques such as sketching and prototypes (see Figure 2.5).

Back to Analysis

Finally, we start over again at the Analysis phase. Remember, the goal is quick and constant iteration. We can—and most likely will—move back and forth around the loop. It is quite common to move between the Analysis and Design phases a few times before going on to the Evaluation phase. There is no wrong way so long as we are constantly iterating and improving based on regular feedback from the users (see Figure 2.6).

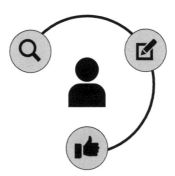

FIGURE 2.5   The Evaluation phase of the User-Centered Design process.

FIGURE 2.6   Returning back to the Analysis phase.

THE POWER OF PRE-VISUALIZATION

One of the most powerful aspects of the User-Centered Design process is pre-visualization, which allows us to learn more about the user experience before we write any code. This helps to ensure that the time spent developing the tools is as efficient as possible.

The decision to invest in these pre-visualization techniques depends on a variety of factors: how complex the change is, the programming resources that are available at the time, and so on. We will discuss this in Chapter 6.

Jeff's Block of Wood

In the mid-1990s, electronic pocket organizers were gaining in popularity. These devices were portable computers designed to replace your address book, calendar, and notepad. The problem was that most of their features were badly implemented, and some were too big to deserve the term "pocket."

Jeff Hawkins was one of the founding members of Palm, and he decided to change that. He and his team started working on a pocket-sized personal organizer that had a limited feature set. Through observation and analysis, Hawkins identified a small set of features that he felt most people wanted a pocket organizer to do really well.

Getting the right size and form factor for a device that fits in your pocket is not easy. When it comes to hardware, you cannot make a change after a device comes off the assembly line. Getting it wrong can be disastrous. Palm did not have unlimited resources to fabricate prototypes.

One day Jeff came in to work with a wood block small enough to be held in one hand. In a meeting, he took out the wood block out and started tapping on it. The next day, he came in with another wood block that was a

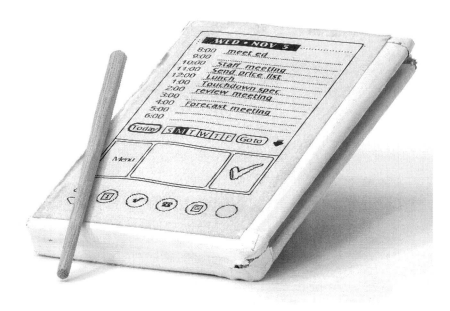

FIGURE 2.7   A prototype of the first Palm Pilot, created by Jeff Hawkins. © Mark Richards. Courtesy of the Computer History Museum.

slightly different size. Approaching a group of people having a discussion, he took out the wood block and pretended to enter someone's information into an address book. The day after that, he came in with a slightly smaller, but thicker wood block. After making plans to meet someone, he took out the wood block and pretended to enter a new meeting in his calendar (see Figure 2.7).

Had he lost his mind? No, quite the opposite.* Jeff was working on finding the right size and form factor early on in the process, in an inexpensive and fast way. Instead of going straight to manufacturing with a design that was untested, he found a way to try out different options in situations similar to those where the real device would be used. Over time, he iterated on the wood blocks to create prototypes that were increasingly sophisticated, complete with an interface printed on paper and a stylus made from a chopstick. When he had arrived at a form factor that felt right, he was able to use the prototypes to help people understand his vision. All of this work contributed to the release of the first Palm Pilot, a device that would

---

* In fact, Jeff Hawkins knows a thing or two about the mind. In addition to being a brilliant innovator, Jeff also has a deep understanding of the brain. In 2004, he wrote a book about how we think, titled *On Intelligence*. Knowing how the brain works is useful information when you are designing for people.

outsell the competition, spawn a long list of imitators, and ultimately have a huge impact on the world of portable electronics.

The important lesson that we can learn from this is that when resources are not available or are too expensive, pre-visualization techniques are one way to allow everyone to have a shared vision of what the tool will be, and understand how it will be used in context, before you start investing resources in development.

Getting the Design Right and the Right Design

When creating a feature for a tool, it is often considered prohibitive to build a few alternatives in an effort to pick the best option. However, the long-term cost of getting the feature wrong can be much higher than taking the time to create a few alternatives! Bill Buxton summarizes this perfectly in the subtitle of his book *Sketching User Experiences*: "Getting the Design Right and the Right Design." It is one thing to get the design right, but make sure you are doing the right design in the first place.

While it is true that Jeff's wood blocks did not have the functionality of a real Palm Pilot, it was enough to help him fail early and often in a quick and inexpensive way. Once he had learned all that he could from that prototype, he was able to share it with other people and move on to more sophisticated prototypes. Pre-visualization can help us do the same for our game development tools.

Having the Same Vision

If you have worked in game development long enough, you may be familiar with this situation: developers and users are gathered in a meeting room, discussing how a tool will work. Users talk about what they need, and developers ask questions. When everyone agrees on what to do, an e-mail is sent out with bullet-points that summarize the decisions. The developers make changes to the tool, and a few days later, the users get their hands on it. The first reaction from the users is, "This isn't what we asked for!" Frustrated, the developers reply, "It is! It's written right here in the e-mail!" When the stakeholders find out about the situation, they say, "Why are the users unable to produce the content we need for the game? Why are the developers saying they need more time to make changes to the tool?" If we do not visualize what we intend to build, there will always be room for interpretation and misunderstanding.

For example, consider the word *Letters* (left side of Figure 2.8). If you were to close your eyes and visualize what that word means to you,

FIGURE 2.8 Without visualization, a word can be interpreted in different ways.

what would you see? A stack of paper letters in envelopes or letters of the alphabet?

When it comes to a topic as complex as the user experience of a game development tool, we need to visualize the meaning of our words. If we do not, there is a good chance that we are not talking about the same thing.

GETTING TO A BETTER USER EXPERIENCE FASTER

Starting Closer

If we could track the development of a tool on a linear time graph, it might look something like the left side of Figure 2.9. The bottom represents time, and the left side represents the target zone for a user experience that is optimally usable, useful, and desirable. Our goal is to hit that zone as closely as possible.*

When we do not design for the right users or fully understand their goals, we start far away from the target zone (represented by the triangle on the right side of Figure 2.9).

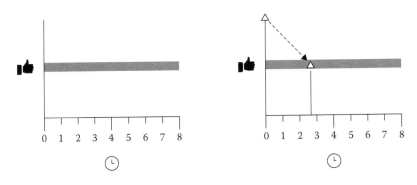

FIGURE 2.9 Starting far from the target zone increases the time it takes to achieve an improved user experience.

---

* The book *Effective UI* by Anderson, McRee, Wilson, et al. uses a very similar graph to compare the slow iteration of the waterfall process versus the fast iteration of Agile.

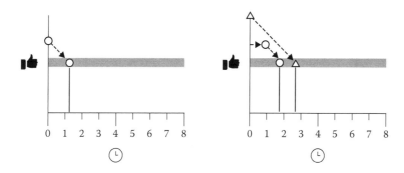

FIGURE 2.10 Starting closer to the target zone means that it takes less time to achieve an improved user experience, even if you take into account the time spent in the User-Centered Design process.

However, if we invest in the Analysis phase of the User-Centered Design process, we start closer. This means that hitting the target zone takes less time (represented by the circle on the left side of Figure 2.10). Even if we start a little bit later because we have chosen to invest time in the Analysis phase, we will still have a better chance of hitting our target zone faster (see the right side of Figure 2.10) because we know what we are building and who we are building it for.

Small, Frequent Iterations

When we do not get feedback from the users on a regular basis, every iteration can result in big, time-consuming changes. Each version attempts to realign the tool to address what the users need, and the degree of success can vary wildly (see the left side of Figure 2.11).

By comparison, the User-Centered Design process emphasizes short, frequent repetitions of the iteration loop: analyze the situation, design one

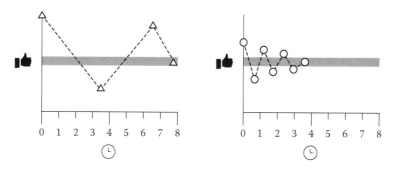

FIGURE 2.11 More frequent iterations allow developers to adapt the user experience faster, and with more confidence.

or more focused improvements, and then evaluate the impact on the user experience. Validating the tool with the users on a regular basis makes for smaller, more concentrated adjustments (see the right side of Figure 2.11). This helps to achieve the goal of an ideal user experience more quickly and efficiently.

INTEGRATING THE USER-CENTERED DESIGN PROCESS INTO AGILE

Emphasizing short, rapid iterations will feel familiar to those who work with the Scrum framework of the Agile software development process. However, despite the similarities between Agile and the User-Centered Design process, it may not be immediately apparent how to integrate the two.

Before Joining the Sprint

At the beginning of the project, it is normal to spend a bit of time gathering information about who the stakeholders and users are before going through the phases of Analysis, Design, and Evaluation.* A frequent reaction to this is, "What do the developers do while that is happening?" The fact is that there will always be programming tasks that can be done during this time, such as work on the back-end, technical investigations, or other things that will not affect the user interface.

Linking to the Sprint

One of the advantages of going through each phase of the User-Centered Design process within a single sprint is that it forces small change and rapid iteration. Here is how each of the phases can be integrated.

Iteration Loop

Once you have a plan, you can set deadlines for the Analysis, Design, and Evaluation phases within the sprint. For example, if the sprint lasts two or three weeks—a common length for many teams—you can set a deadline to complete the Analysis phase before the first third, the Design phase before the second third, and finally, the Evaluation phase before the end of the sprint (see Figure 2.12).

---

* In their article "Adapting Usability Investigations for Agile User-Centered Design" for the *Journal of Usability Studies*, authors Desiree Sy and Lynn Miller call this "Cycle 0." You can read it here: http://www.upassoc.org/upa_publications/jus/2007may/agile-ucd.pdf.

FIGURE 2.12   Integrating the User-Centered Design process within a single sprint.

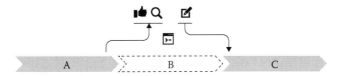

FIGURE 2.13   Integrating the User-Centered Design process across several sprints.

More Complex Designs

In the case of bigger, more complex features that take more than a week to design, there are other approaches to integrating the iteration loop into the sprint.

One approach is to prepare designs one sprint in advance, and dedicate an entire sprint to implementation. For example, consider Figure 2.13, which shows three consecutive sprints. During sprint B, developers are implementing the changes from the previous Design phase. Meanwhile, the people in charge of the User-Centered Design process do the Evaluation phase on the latest build of the tool from sprint A. Then, they look at the results in the Analysis phase. Finally, changes are proposed in the Design phase and delivered right before the start of sprint C, and then the cycle shifts ahead by one sprint.

WHO HAS THE TIME TO DO ALL OF THIS?

This process might seem like a lot of work. For many, this is a big shift away from how tools development is traditionally done. However, if we agree that the way we have been working in the past has resulted in tools with a bad user experience, perhaps it is time to try something different. Working differently will require a culture shift, which we will discuss in the final chapter.

In a perfect world, there would be one person in each tools team driving the User-Centered Design process. However, when that is not possible, the team must work together and take it upon themselves to apply these concepts in an effort to show that improving the user experience is a worthy investment.

If you studied object-oriented programming in school, you probably started by creating class diagrams. If you studied 3D modeling, you probably started by using a front and side reference drawing. After a few years of programming, you no longer needed to create a class diagram for every single class, and you no longer needed front and side references to create every single model. They were useful tools in the early days, but as you gained more experience, you internalized the process and started intuitively applying the concepts and techniques without needing a guide.

That is how you can apply the User-Centered Design process presented in this book. Start by using it as a guide. Once you have applied the principles long enough, it will naturally become part of your development process. That is when you will begin to see big improvements to the user experience of your tools.

WRAPPING UP

In this chapter, we learned about the User-Centered Design process and how it can help us achieve a better user experience. We also learned how pre-visualization can be used in certain situations to help us improve our design and allow everyone involved to have the same vision of what we are going to build. Finally, we discussed how the User-Centered Design process can be integrated into Agile and how to justify the time and resources.

In the next chapter, we will learn what it means to be "User-Centered," which is one of the most important aspects of improving the user experience of game development tools.

CHAPTER 3

What Does It Mean to Be "User-Centered"?

WHAT WILL WE LEARN IN THIS CHAPTER?

- The importance of starting with the users
- How to focus on the right users
- Understanding the difference between features and goals
- Doing one thing really well
- Why it is important to choose the right features

START WITH THE USERS

> "You've got to start with the customer experience and work back toward the technology—not the other way around."
>
> —STEVE JOBS

THAT STATEMENT, MADE IN 1996 by the late CEO of Apple while he was hosting an open question-and-answer session,* would define a new direction for the company. It would also take their shares from the rock bottom price of four dollars to over 600 dollars in a little over a decade.

---

* The full video can be seen here: "Steve Jobs on Apple Customer Experience and Innovation," https://www.youtube.com/watch?v=1SIeTmORl0E.

Google clearly seems to share this mindset. On the corporate section of their webpage that lists their philosophies, one reads "Focus on the user and all else will follow."* That mentality has also helped take them from a small start-up to the world leader in search.

We Are Not the Users

If you are involved in the creation of game development tools, take a minute to ask yourself these questions:

- Who are the people using the tools to produce final content for the game?

- Who uses the tools all day (and even late into the night)?

- Whose job depends on how well they can use the tools?

If you are referring to software used to program game development tools (such as Microsoft Visual Studio, Eclipse, and Apple Xcode) or design the interfaces for game development tools (such as Adobe Photoshop, Microsoft Expression Blend, and Qt Designer), then the answer is you. However, if you are talking about anything else, then there is only one answer: the users!

One of the biggest mistakes that we make as game tools developers is creating tools without first understanding the people who use them. We can assume that we know the goals of the users and the context in which they use the tools. Some of us may not see this as a problem because we have worked this way for years.† Changing this view is one of the first steps on the road to improving the user experience of our game development tools.

We need to accept that we do not always know the answers to these questions. Furthermore, we need to make it part of our job to find out—even if we have many years of experience in the industry, even if we have previously worked in the same position, or even if we have a good relationship with someone who does now. Our opinion, or that of one or two expert users, does not represent the reality of everyone using the tools to produce the majority of the game's content.

---

* This comes from the Google company philosophy page, "Ten Things We Know to Be True," http://www.google.ca/about/company/philosophy/.
† Including myself!

When we learn about the users, we must also share what we have learned with everyone involved in the development of the tool. If everyone shares the same vision of whom a tool is being developed for, they are better prepared to work as a team to build a great user experience.

What Happens When We Do Not Know Whom We Are Designing For?

When we do not know whom a tool is for, we end up creating a tool for everyone. There is an old saying about that: "When you try to please everyone, you please no one."

What does that mean in the context of game development tools? Consider the following scenario: Three people are working together to create a game development tool. Based on their own experiences, each one has a different view of who uses the tool, what they need, and how they use it. They do not have a shared vision of whom they are building for. They combine their ideas together into one big list of features.

The first person adds a few initial features (left side of Figure 3.1). Then, the second person adds a few more features, because they have a different view of what the users need (middle of Figure 3.1). Finally, the third person adds more features as well, based on their view of what the users need (right side of Figure 3.1).

Once you see this, you begin to understand why some users say that their game development tools are overly complicated and difficult to learn!

Documentation Is Not the Magic Solution

It might seem logical to expect users to read the documentation before saying that tool is hard to understand. That would be true, if the documentation is up to date, or if it even exists. When it does exist, how many people actually read it end to end? Often it is the technical directors, technical artists, and tools developers who act as the documentation. They are also a

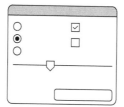

FIGURE 3.1 Trying to create an interface to "please everyone" usually results in an interface that will "please no one."

single point of failure (What if they are run over by a Warthog tomorrow?). In addition, if there are people constantly asking them questions about how to use the tools, they have less time to solve other big problems.

A user manual is important and should be created and maintained if the resources are available, but we also need to do our best to create tools where the basic functionality is easy to learn without requiring the user to read a manual.

Stop the Culture of "RTFM"

On the topic of manuals, one of the biggest challenges to improving the user experience of game development tools is the culture of "RTFM": blaming the user when they do something wrong. Content creators are good at creating content. That is already a very big responsibility and can take years of hard work! Not only is it unrealistic for us to expect the users to understand everything technical related to game development, it can also be seen as hostile. This hurts communication and teamwork. Instead of blaming the users or expecting them to become something that they are not, we need to start understanding them.

FOCUS ON THE RIGHT USERS

As we learned earlier, when we try to please everyone, we please no one. However, the opposite can also be true: it can be problematic to design for only one or two people.*

In the case of a tool that is made to be used by a lot of users with minimal technical knowledge, designing for one or two people who are highly technical and do not use the tools very often can make this situation worse. For example, consider that all of the users of a tool are spread among the following two axes: technical knowledge and frequency of use (see the left side of Figure 3.2). If we only talk to the users in the upper left who are more technical and do not use the tool very often (for example, to set up a pipeline or train a new user), we are missing the opinions of a large percentage of the user base.

The key is to work with enough users so we know the majority of the users' needs (highlighted area on the right of Figure 3.2) and to work with users who represent the mix of people using the tool (highlighted area on the left of Figure 3.2), so we are not trying to please everyone at once.

---

* Malcolm Gladwell discusses this effect, known as the inverted U-curve, in his book *David & Goliath: Underdogs, Misfits, and the Art of Battling Giants.*

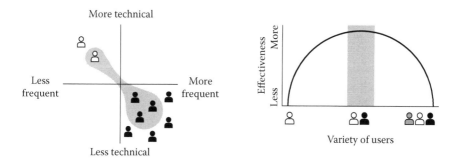

FIGURE 3.2   Focusing on the right users: finding the right balance.

Minimal Investment for Maximum Results

Earlier, we spoke about the benefits of saving 20 minutes per 8-hour day for 20 users. Let us imagine that instead we found a way to save 30 minutes a day. This sounds like a great improvement. However, the impact changes if that savings is only for five users, instead of 20. Alternatively, imagine if those users actually use the tool only two hours per day, instead of all eight hours per day. To make matters worse, if our savings of 30 minutes comes from the implementation of a complex new feature that only five people use, we have also spent a lot of time and money on development. This is a lose/lose scenario (see the left side of Figure 3.3).

We can also imagine another scenario where we save time for 50 users. This sounds like we are helping a large number of people! However, because we tried to please everyone, we spent a lot of time implementing too many features and did not have the time to optimize them. As a result, we only save each user one minute per day. Even though it seems that we are making things better, we are saving less overall (see the middle of Figure 3.3).

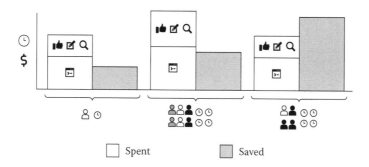

FIGURE 3.3   How focusing on the right users can maximize the improvement to the user experience, for a minimal investment.

Instead, we need to find the people who are using the tools for the most number of hours in the day and focus on delivering a focused feature set that satisfies their needs (see the right side of Figure 3.3). This will give us the maximum results for the minimum investment.

We're Not Going to Make Everyone Happy

It is important to keep in mind that we are not going to make everyone happy. We have to look at the big picture. We are going to make the most frequent users more productive. That will result in the biggest impact on the user experience overall.

FEATURES VERSUS GOALS

If you have worked in a game tools development team, at some point you have heard someone say, "Why don't the users know what they want? Why can't they just tell us?" In addition, you may be familiar with the perception that when a user is asked if they want a feature, nine times out of ten they will say yes, regardless of the priority or usefulness.

Both of these situations highlight the problems that occur when we focus on features instead of user goals. One important point that we need to understand is this: it is not the user's job to design the user interface. However, it is their job to be able to tell us what their goals are!

Swiss Army Knife Compared to Scissors

To understand this better, let us consider two common tools: a Swiss army knife and pair of scissors (see Figure 3.4).

The Swiss army knife is a great invention. Hidden inside the average Swiss army knife is a multitude of tools, from simple cutting blades to

FIGURE 3.4   Features versus goals: comparing a Swiss army knife to scissors.

corkscrews, mini-scissors, toothpicks, bottle openers, and more. Swiss army knives do a lot of great stuff. There are two trade-offs, though: First, because they do such a great variety of things, they are not necessarily very good at any one thing in particular. Second, if you have never used a Swiss army knife before, it is not immediately clear how it works at first glance, or the variety of tools contained within.

Now, let us compare that to a pair of scissors. Scissors do one thing really well: they cut paper! However, they are not good at much else. If we needed to open a bottle, and all we had was a pair of scissors, we would be out of luck. However, for cutting paper, scissors are hard to beat. Unlike the Swiss army knife, however, they are much more intuitive: The two holes suggest where we should place our fingers. They can only move in one axis. They do not hide their functionality. They are never in a specific "mode."

Understand What the User Is Trying to Accomplish

How does this relate to features versus goals? The truth is that many of our tools resemble the Swiss army knife: they do many things, but they tend to do those things moderately well from the user's perspective. It is also not clear what they do just by looking at them. This is because we pack them with features without always understanding what the majority of the users' goals are.

If the user's goal is to cut a piece of paper in half, and we give them the option of either a Swiss army knife or a pair of scissors, the scissors would be the clear choice. This illustrates the importance of understanding the user's goals. Before we start adding features, we need to understand what the user is trying to accomplish. By knowing this, we can design the right tool for the task.

A Faster Horse

When asked about the invention of the automobile, it is widely believed that Henry Ford said, "If I had asked people what they wanted, they would have said faster horses!" This quote is often used to suggest that you cannot create innovative products if you ask the users or stakeholders what they want.

As it turns out, Henry Ford never actually said that.* However, he did say this: "If there is any one secret of success, it lies in the ability to get the

---

* No references to this quote can be found in books, in web searches, and even from the historians at the Ford Museum: http://blogs.hbr.org/2011/08/henry-ford-never-said-the-fast/.

other person's point of view and see things from that person's angle as well as from your own."

Learning about people and their goals is not the same thing as letting them design the features. If you understand what people need, you are in a much better position to propose features that address those goals.

In other words, the user is the best person to tell you that they want to go from point A to point B. Once you understand that, you can suggest a faster horse or an automobile.

DO ONE THING REALLY WELL

"Good design is as little design as possible."

—DIETER RAMS

Another philosophy listed on the Google company webpage is this: "It's best to do one thing really, really well." Google decided early on that their focus would be search. Although they went on to create a variety of different services, search has always been at their core. They have chosen not to do some other things so that they can allocate the necessary resources to continue providing the best search experience.

Being Proud of the Things We Haven't Done

Another one of the philosophies that transformed Apple into a huge success after the turn of the millennium was focusing on a few key products and features. That attitude is perfectly represented in this quote from Steve Jobs: "I'm as proud of the things we haven't done as the things we have done."

It is important to note that saying "no" does not mean, "We'll never do this." It means "not yet." Knowing what not to do helps you prioritize. One of the best ways to know what not to do is to know who your users are and what they need.

We are often overwhelmed by the number of features that we feel must be added to a tool. There is never enough time to add everything, and the priorities are always changing. However, if we are asking ourselves, "How are we going to create all of these features before the deadline?" perhaps we are not asking the right question. Instead, perhaps we should start by asking ourselves, "Are these the right features?"

This mentality is also reflected in another quote from Mr. Jobs, this time while speaking at WWDC 1997: "The line of code that is the fastest to write, that never breaks, that never needs maintenance, is the line that you never have to write."

The Monkeys and the Banana

We have a tendency to support features simply because we have always done so. If we have built or used a tool in the past with a certain list of features, and it worked for the users at the time, we assume that we need those features.

This behavior is similar to the story of the monkeys and the banana (see Figure 3.5). Imagine that there are three monkeys in a room. At one point, a banana is placed in the room. One of the monkeys walks over to the banana and picks it up. At that moment, a door on the ceiling opens and a bucket of water is dumped on the other two monkeys in the room. All of the moneys are wet, except for the one who took the banana, who is happily munching away. Naturally, the other monkeys—now, soaking wet—are not thrilled.

Later, another banana is placed in the room. The same thing happens: one of the monkeys takes the banana, and the other monkeys get soaking wet. The monkeys start to understand that when one monkey gets the banana, the other monkeys are in for a bad time.

The next time a banana is placed in the room and one of the monkeys reaches for it, the other monkeys beat him up before he can get to it. Soon enough, all of the monkeys are afraid of going near the bananas.

Now, imagine that we take one of the monkeys out of the room and replace it with another one who has never been in the room before. When a banana is placed in the room, the new monkey will naturally attempt to get it. This is when the other monkeys, knowing what will happen to them, pile on the new monkey and beat him up. The new monkey is terrified and does not understand why the others are so angry!

Over time, imagine that we replace all of the monkeys in the room so that all of the original monkeys are gone. The monkeys in the room know

FIGURE 3.5 The analogy of the monkeys and the banana.

that the rule is "No one goes near the bananas," but they do not know why. That is just the way it is.

This is why we sometimes add features or design tools in a certain way without questioning it: "We've just always done it this way." However, we have to ask ourselves, are all of those features necessary?

CHOOSE THE RIGHT FEATURES

To understand what is necessary, we need to understand the needs of the people using the tools. If we do not do this, we may end up trying to deliver too much at once or work on things that the users do not need right away. All of this leaves us with less time to create a great user experience for the things that the users really do need.

Less of What You Don't Need, More of What You Do

In the early 2000s, laptop makers were struggling to find ways to make their laptops lighter while still packing in all of the common components, such as a disc drive. They never questioned the disc drive, because "we've just always done it this way."

Meanwhile, Apple took a step back and observed that very few people still use disc drives on a regular basis. As a result, they started phasing out disc drives on all of their devices. Now, if you absolutely need a disc drive, you buy an external one.

This focus has not only allowed them to make their laptops lighter than the competition (see Figure 3.6), but they were able to fill up some of that extra space with a larger battery. They determined that increased battery life is a feature that people find more compelling than having a disc drive. As is the case with other disruptive decisions that Apple has made, we now see other companies following their lead and removing disc drives in favor of larger batteries.

Before you decide what to work on first, make certain that all of the features are useful for the majority of users and therefore important enough to justify your efforts. If your schedule treats features that will be useful for 80 percent of users equal to those made for one or two expert users,* then perhaps those priorities need to be challenged.

---

* As long as the feature is not a key element related to setting up a pipeline, which could result in a bottleneck for the rest of the content creators.

FIGURE 3.6 While other manufacturers were constrained with the assumption that all laptops must have a disc drive (bottom), Apple observed that very few people used their laptop disc drives, and decided to use that space to make a thinner laptop with better battery life (top).

More Features Do Not Make a Better Tool

The Apple iPod is another excellent example of this philosophy. The biggest competitor to the third-generation iPod was the iRiver H300. At the time, iRiver was a rising star in the MP3 player market. Their H300 had many impressive features. It supported a large number of file formats: Not only could it play music from MP3, WMA, and OGG files, but it could also play videos and view pictures. It had an FM tuner, two headphone jacks, and a color display, just to name a few unique features. How did the third-generation iPod compare to this? It only played music. It did not have an FM tuner. It had one headphone jack. The display was black and white. The iPod had fewer features, by far. (See Figure 3.7.) However, not only did the iPod outsell the H300, it also outsold every other MP3 player on the market. Perhaps most telling is the fact that very few people talk about iRiver these days.

FIGURE 3.7 The third-generation iPod (left) compared to the iRivier H300 (right).

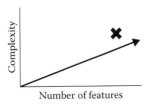 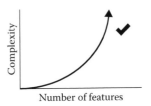

FIGURE 3.8   Adding more features increases complexity exponentially.

How did Apple do this? Several factors contributed to the success of the iPod, but one thing is certain: it was not by having more features. Apple focused all their resources on the right features, to give the iPod the best user experience possible. Products that choose the right features, and do them well, are in a much better position to succeed.

Exponential Complexity

We may believe that adding features makes a product more complex in a linear fashion. However, the fact is that each new feature increases complexity exponentially. (See Figure 3.8.) This is because every feature will be used in combination with all of the other existing features, which adds an extra dimension to all those that came before it. This is why it is of the utmost importance to choose the right features, and choose them carefully.

WRAPPING UP

In this chapter, we discussed the value of increasing the involvement of users in the development process. We discussed the importance of accepting that—more often than not—we are not the users, as well as the dangers of not knowing for whom we are designing. We also learned that documentation is not the magic solution and why it's important to stop the culture of "RTFM." In addition, we learned how focusing on the right users allows us to get the maximum results from a minimal investment, accepting that we're not going to make everyone happy. Finally, we learned the difference between features and goals, the fact that more features do not make a tool better, and why understanding the goals of the users can help us choose the right features.

In the next chapter, we will learn important concepts and techniques that we can use during the Analysis phase of the User-Centered Design process.

CHAPTER 4

Analysis

WHAT WILL WE LEARN IN THIS CHAPTER?

Concepts

- The importance of watching users work

- Introduction to human–computer interaction

- Understanding the mental model of the users

Techniques

- Interviewing stakeholders

- Performing a contextual analysis

- How to create a task flow

- How to discover the mental models of the users

- Establishing how to measure improvements to the tools

THE IMPORTANCE OF WATCHING USERS WORK

Jakob Nielsen is one of the principals of the respected usability consultancy Nielsen Norman Group (of which Don Norman is also a principal). One of his more famous articles is on the importance of watching users work. In his article, he writes, "To discover which designs work best, watch users as they attempt to perform tasks with the user interface."* It is

---

* The full article can be found here: http://www.nngroup.com/articles/first-rule-of-usability-dont-listen-to-users/.

not enough to simply ask the users about how they use the tool. There are aspects of the user's world in the heat of production that are impossible to understand unless you sit next to them and watch them work.

The Limitations of Metrics and Focus Groups

Two of the most common techniques that we may use to understand how people work are metrics and focus groups. Unfortunately, sometimes we base much of our tools development decisions on these techniques without actually sitting down with the users watching them work. This can have serious implications.

Metrics are a quantitative technique that make it easier to get information about a large number of people. Metrics are very good at telling us what is happening but not very good at telling us why it is happening. When the metrics report that 90 percent of the users never click a specific button, we have no idea why they are not clicking on it. The users may have a very good reason that we cannot be aware of unless we watch the users work: for example, they may not understand the label, or the button may be hidden behind another window.

In a focus group, the loudest and more influential person will usually be heard above everyone else. Even if many other people in the room have an opinion, or actually use the tool more hours per week, their voices are not heard. Furthermore, Jakob Nielsen's research suggests that what people say they do compared to what they actually do is often quite different.

Metrics and focus groups can be great starting points, but they should be complemented by sitting down with the users and watching them work.

Proximity to the Users

Outside of the games industry, having users nearby that you can watch is considered a luxury! Many companies spend astronomical amounts of money getting access to users so they can ask them for feedback on their products. They may pay for transportation, food, and even cash or a gift card as incentive for people to participate. They might also pay an online service to find users and do the analysis for them.

Game developers who work in the same building as their users are at a huge advantage to improve the user experience of their tools. They can talk to their users on a regular basis and have a very tight iteration loop. If this is your situation, you should make the most of it and sit as close as possible to the users.

There are some situations where there are users available, but the developers do not have easy access to them. Some examples of this are if you work for a middle-ware company, or the users are in another building or even another country. In this case, you can use remote collaboration tools such as WebEx, GoToMeeting, and LiveMeeting. They provide features that make it easier to talk to users and get feedback on your tools.

If you are an independent tools developer, you can try to find users with the right profile in online chat forums, such as the CGSociety forums or PolyCount. Many people who participate in online communities would jump at the opportunity to try out a new tool or to give their opinion on how they would use it.

Uncovering Work-Arounds

Watching users work is also a great way to uncover work-arounds. After using a tool for a long time, users forget that they do certain things automatically, which could potentially result in reduced productivity. The story of the monkeys and the banana from Chapter 3 is a perfect example of this behavior.

When you see the user doing something that seems like a work-around, try asking them why. Every time you ask why, you dig deeper into the root of the problem. For example, imagine this exchange between you and a user:

User: "So, first I'll choose a new object from this list. Before I do that, I have to press F5." <user waits>

You: "OK. While we're waiting, can you tell me why you do that?"

User: "Oh, pressing F5 refreshes the list so I see all of the latest objects."

You: "Why do you do that?"

User: "Just in case someone added a new object since the last time I opened the list."

You: "Why are the new objects not added to the list automatically?"

User: "That's a good question. I don't know … It's just always been that way!"

Understanding Context

More often than not, tools are made to work with other tools, and assets are passed around between multiple users. Because of this, it is essential to understand the context in which the tools are used. Taking a step back and seeing the big picture can make the difference between a bad user experience and a good one.

Jeff Hawkins understood this while experimenting with his wood block. He learned some of the different situations in which the Palm Pilot would be used: in the context of a meeting, at a discussion around the watercooler, and when bumping into someone. He thought beyond just the interface of the device. He understood that after using their Palm Pilots to store information, people would want to return to their computers and be able to access the contacts and appointments that they added. This realization led to the ability to easily charge and synchronize your device with your computer, which was crucial to the success of Palm.

By being aware of context, Apple was able to think beyond how people listen to music, and understand how people want to get music onto their devices. This led to the creation of iTunes, one of the biggest selling points of the iPod and a huge source of income for Apple.

The information that we learn in the Analysis phase can be invaluable for understanding context, which can have a huge impact on improving the user experience.

What Is the Problem That We Are Trying to Solve?

In addition to uncovering work-arounds, watching users work also helps us to remember the problem that tool was originally made to solve. When a tool has been used in production for a while, we may try to find solutions that conform to the existing interface. This tunnel vision can hinder our ability to improve the user experience.

For example, imagine that you are working on a shader creation tool for texture artists. The majority of beginner users are having trouble understanding that when they want transparency, they need to check the "Alpha On" checkbox on the shader options. In addition, the checkbox is hidden among a long list of variables in the Options tab for the shader. It takes several clicks to enable, which hurts the efficiency of the users.

We might think that the solution would be to rename the label from "Alpha On" to "Enable Alpha Transparency" so it is clearer for beginners, or to reduce the number of clicks required to get to the checkbox. These are both good ideas, but we must always ask ourselves, "What is the problem that we are trying to solve?" Our goal is not to make a better checkbox, or a clearer label. What we really want to do is make it easier to enable alpha transparency on the shader!

Instead, we could automatically activate transparency when the texture map in the diffuse input has an alpha channel. The diffuse texture needs to have an alpha channel anyway! This solves the real problem and is much more effective than a clearer label or better checkbox placement. Furthermore, this also results in one less checkbox for the tools developers to maintain, and one less checkbox for the user to learn.

INTRODUCTION TO HUMAN–COMPUTER INTERACTION

Tools developers are very familiar with using software and hardware to receive an input, process it, and then send an output. For example, a computer receives input from the mouse, calculates what should happen, and then displays the result on the monitor (see the right side of Figure 4.1, clockwise from top).

Although we may be familiar with the computer side, not everyone understands what is going on inside the user's head while we are watching them work. As it turns out, the human side is almost a mirror image of the computer side: we receive an input, we process it, and then we send an output. For example, we see what is on the monitor, we think about what it means, and then we click the mouse. After our mouse click changes what we see on the monitor, we start back at the beginning (see the left side of Figure 4.1, clockwise from bottom). This communication loop is called the *human–computer interaction model*, and understanding it is key to improving the user experience.

Finally, in between the human and the computer is the user interface (see the middle of Figure 4.1). The quality of the interface determines how good the interaction between the human and the computer will be.

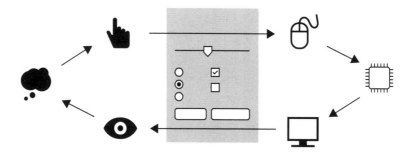

FIGURE 4.1   The quality of the interaction between the user (left) and the computer (right) is determined by the interface (middle).

Understanding the Action Cycle

The communication loop on the human side can be boiled down to three phases: "Look," "Think," and "Act." This is sometimes called the "Action Cycle."*

Imagine for a moment that you had never used a computer mouse before. If you were told to move the cursor on a computer screen using the Logitech MK710 Wireless Desktop Mouse for the first time, you might start by looking at the shape of the mouse: along the left side, there is a deep groove, and the top has two shallower grooves. Then you might think to yourself, "If I were to hold this object, my thumb would fit into that deep groove, and my fingers would drape over the shallower grooves."† Finally, you would act by placing your hand over the mouse and perhaps moving it a bit. Finally, the cycle would start back from the beginning: look at the screen, and think to yourself, "What changed? Oh, the cursor moved!"

With enough experience, you no longer need to look at the mouse to see where the grooves are, or think about what they mean. You spend almost all of your time in the act phase of the action cycle. The fact that the look and think phases are reduced means you can spend more time acting, resulting in increased efficiency (see Figure 4.2).

The Logitech mouse has been designed to be easy to understand so you can start using it immediately. However, not all computer mice are designed this way. For instance, consider the Mad Catz R.A.T. mouse (see Figure 4.3). For someone who has never used a mouse before, the shape

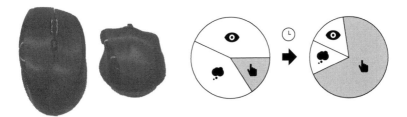

FIGURE 4.2 The design of a mouse can make it easier to learn, reducing the time spent in the Action Cycle.

---

* The action cycle is part of the field of action research, pioneered in the 1940s by Kurt Lewin, a professor at MIT. According to Lewin, humans constantly iterate through three phases when performing actions: planning, acting, and evaluating the results. More recently, Don Norman proposed a "Human Action Cycle" more geared toward human–computer interaction, which features three very similar phases: goal forming, execution, and evaluation.

† When the shape of an object suggests how you should interact with it, this is called "Affordance," which you can read more about here: http://en.wikipedia.org/wiki/Affordance.

FIGURE 4.3 A non-standard or confusing design can increase the amount of time spent in the Action Cycle.

does not make it immediately obvious how you are supposed to hold it. It also has different modes, which means that it works differently depending on what mode the mouse is in. Another example is a novelty computer mouse, especially those that are made to look like other objects like cars or sports equipment. If the user is unfamiliar with what a mouse is, they will likely spend a lot more time in the look phase trying to understand what they are seeing. All of this wasted time could be spent in the act phase. Novelty mice are a good example of devices that have the useful and desirable layer of the pyramid but are missing the usable layer.

Mental Loads

Susan Weinschenk's book *100 Things Every Designer Needs to Know about People* presents the concept of loads, which are the three types of processes that the brain can perform: cognitive, visual, and motor. She describes them as follows: "There are things you're thinking about and remembering (cognitive), things you're looking at on the screen (visual), and buttons you are pressing, mouse movements, and typing (motor)."

She goes on to reveal that not all loads are processed equally. Visual loads require more resources to process than motor loads. Cognitive loads require more resources than visual loads. Therefore, the hierarchy of loads—from most to least resources required—is cognitive, then visual, and finally, motor (see Figure 4.4).

How does this relate to the action cycle? When you are in the look phase, you are processing a visual load. When you are in the think phase,

FIGURE 4.4 The hierarchy of mental loads, from lightest to heaviest: motor, visual, and cognitive.

you are processing a cognitive load. Finally, when you are in the act phase, you are processing a motor load. If a tool has a complicated user interface (visual load), the user will spend a lot of time in the look phase. If the tool requires that the user do a lot of mental calculation and remember things (cognitive load), the user will spend a lot of time in the think phase. This is made worse by the fact that cognitive and visual loads are more time consuming to process compared to motor loads.

More Clicks Are Not Always Bad

Common sense tells us that adding a hundred clicks to a task is going to reduce efficiency. However, it may come as a surprise to find that adding just a few extra clicks—resulting in a slightly increased motor load—can actually increase efficiency. How can this be?

Susan Weinschenk supports this by describing research she did comparing different mental loads. Although the users in her research study had to "go through more than 10 clicks to get the task done," they concluded that the task was easy, because "each step was logical and gave them what they expected. They didn't have to think."

Steve Krug, another well-respected author in the field of user experience, is probably best known for his book *Don't Make Me Think*. The topic of the book is exactly that: the less we have to think, the more time we spend acting, and therefore the more efficient we can be. He further confirms Susan Weinschenk's research, stating, "It doesn't matter how many times I have to click, as long as each click is a mindless, unambiguous choice."

How Does the Action Cycle Affect Efficiency?

To see how the action cycle applies to improving the efficiency of game development tools, we will walk through an example. In Chapter 1, we calculated how saving 20 game developers 20 minutes per day could save time

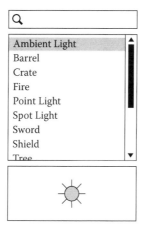

FIGURE 4.5   Example of the interface for a tool used to place objects in a level.

and money. Imagine that those 20 users are placing objects in a level, using a standard level editor. The steps are as follows:

- Look: The user scans the list of objects in the object library.

- Think: Based on what they see, the user determines if they have found the object they need.

- Act: Once the desired object is found, they select it from the list and place it in the level.

The user interface could use the search box at the top, but in this case, the user does not know the name of the object they are looking for (see Figure 4.5). They will know it when they see it. They know that the object can be smashed into pieces by the hero. It is not equipment, a light, or a particle effect. How can the look, think, and act phases be optimized so that the user can find the object that they are looking for?[*]

Look

In the current interface for the object library, there are many different types of objects. It can be difficult for the user to distinguish between various object types at a glance. How can we reduce the time spent in the look phase?

---

[*] In the example that follows, the design techniques of hierarchy, progressive disclosure, representation, grouping, feed-forward, constraints, and excise are being applied. We will learn more about them in Chapter 5.

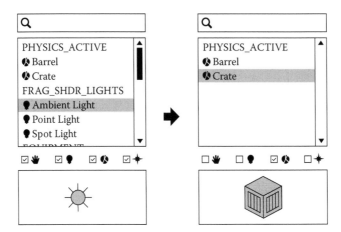

FIGURE 4.6 Improving the user experience to reduce time spent in the look phase.

We could start by improving the way in which the objects are organized so that the categories are easier to distinguish, and then use a unique color and icon for each object type. These changes will make it easier for the user to identify the object they are looking for.

We could also add the ability to filter the list by object type, reducing the number of objects that the user has to scan at once. This does add an additional click, but remember that sometimes adding clicks can actually reduce time spent in the look phase, thereby making the user more efficient overall (see Figure 4.6).

Think

The names of the object categories are taken from the data structures underneath. However, the average user is not aware of that, and so they do not think about the categories in the same way. For example, "Breakables" is a much more common name for the average user of this tool, compared to "Physics_Active." By understanding how they would group the objects together, we can have category names that will allow the user to find what they are looking for more quickly (see the left side of Figure 4.7).

In addition, some objects can only be placed in certain areas of the level (for example, only boats can be placed in water zones). The user has to think about this beforehand; otherwise the object cannot be placed. By showing a semi-grayed-out version of the object when it is being dragged on top of a non-valid zone, the user does not have to spend a lot of time in

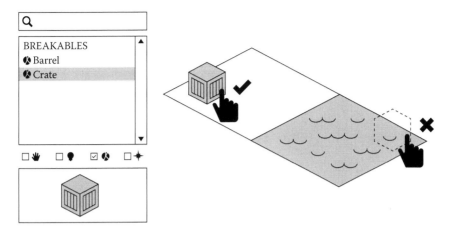

FIGURE 4.7 Improving the user experience to reduce time spent in the think phase.

the think phase, wondering if they are placing the object in the right spot (see the right side of Figure 4.7).

Act

By reducing the look and the think phases with the techniques mentioned above, we can spend more time in the act phase: in other words, placing objects in the level. However, that does not mean that we cannot also optimize the act phase itself!

We can see that having the category filters below the list means a lot of mouse movement up and down. Moving them up between the search field and the list means less travel for the mouse (see the left side of Figure 4.8).

We can also add keyboard shortcuts: one for putting the cursor in the search field, and one for each of the categories to toggle them on and off (see the right side of Figure 4.8).

All of these improvements in combination help to reduce the time spent in the look, think, and act phases. This makes it much more efficient for the user to find the object they are looking for and add it to the level.

How Does the Action Cycle Affect Learnability?

A tool is considered to have good learnability if a new user can easily accomplish a task on the first attempt. The learnability of a tool can also be assessed on a long-term basis: the speed at which an existing user can

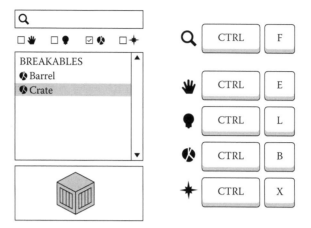

FIGURE 4.8   Improving the user experience to reduce time spent in the act phase.

remember how to use a tool after not having used it for a while (sometimes called *memorability*), or how quickly a beginner can become an expert.*

Other than experimentation, the two most common ways that a new user learns a game development tool are being trained by an expert user and reading documentation. However, there are issues with both of these approaches.

While support from expert users is common, too much can come at a cost. Any time that an expert user spends providing training and answering questions is time that they could be doing what expert users do best: solving complicated problems! Not to mention, the hourly wage for an expert user can be high. Finally, they are not always available: if a new user does not know how to do something without the help of an expert user, they are stuck.

Documentation is always an option, but it is frequently out of date, if it exists at all. It also goes without saying that it can be expensive to create and maintain good documentation.

Do It the Long Way

Experts spend less time in the think phase because they have a deeper understanding of how a tool works. However, if a tool is difficult to learn, users may stay as beginners or intermediates for a long time.

---

* For more on how Nielsen and others define learnability, see here: http://www.measuringusability. com/blog/measure-learnability.php.

This situation is described perfectly in Jeff Johnson's book *Designing with the Mind in Mind*. In his book, he tells a story about a usability test where he asked a user to perform a task. After thinking for a minute, the user told him, "I'm in a hurry ... so I'll do it the long way." This seems like an unusual statement ... or is it?

If you observe how people use game development tools, it is common to see that once they learn how to accomplish a task in a specific way without crashing or causing any other problems they tend to stick to it. This method could contain a ton of work-arounds and hacks, but they know that it works. If the tool makes it difficult to figure out a better way on their own, they are likely to stick to the old way. Now, imagine that there is a newer, better way, but the user cannot find it. Their slower approach takes an additional 20 minutes per day. How much time and money could we save by making this tool more learnable?

Ramping Up the Learning Curve

Understanding what the user needs at each step of their learning process is crucial to designing a tool that is easy to learn by beginners and efficient to use by experts. This also has a relationship to the action cycle: beginners spend a lot more time in the think phase, because they are still figuring out how the tool works. By making it easier for beginners to become experts, they will spend less time in the think phase, making them more efficient.

Imagine a scenario with Microsoft Word. A beginner who has never used Word before may look at the interface and ask, "What can this do?" They may see the "Font" section, and see that it contains buttons for bold, italic, and underline. By looking at the icons, reading the tooltips, and experimenting with the buttons, they start to understand that one of the things Word does is format text (see Figure 4.9).

FIGURE 4.9 The commands exposed in the ribbon help beginners understand what the tool can do. Used with permission from Microsoft.

FIGURE 4.10 Contextual menus allow intermediate users to work more efficiently. Used with permission from Microsoft.

Intermediate users already know that they can format text in Word. They also know that by right-clicking on some text, they get a contextual menu with easy access to the buttons in the Font section. The contextual menu is not visible all the time. It is convenient for the intermediate user, but it does not clutter up the interface (see Figure 4.10).

An expert user of Word also knows that they can format text, and they want to do it as quickly as possible. Since they have learned the hotkeys for bold, italic, and underline, they never use the ribbon. In fact, they have chosen to hide it, thereby customizing their interface and allowing them to focus on their content (see Figure 4.11).

What is important to note here is that if we removed the ribbon, the beginner user would never see the Font section, and it would take longer for them to understand how to format text, blocking their progress toward becoming expert users. However, if there were no hotkeys, the experts would be less efficient and frustrated by having to move their mouse up to the ribbon to access the bold, italics, and underline buttons. These different user interface elements exist to help guide the beginner to becoming an expert.

FIGURE 4.11 Expert users can customize the interface and use hotkeys, maximizing the space used to display their content. Used with permission from Microsoft.

Keep in mind that the expert user's needs mostly apply to complex productivity tools with deep functionality. A simple game development tool with two buttons and a checkbox—such as an installer—is unlikely to require the user to go past the criteria of the beginner or intermediate stage.

Knowledge in the World and Knowledge in the Head

In his book *The Design of Everyday Things*, Don Norman compares two types of knowledge: knowledge in the world and knowledge in the head. Knowledge in the world could be compared to what you see in the user interface, and knowledge in the head could be the equivalent of knowing what a tool does already. Norman suggests that when the functionality we are looking for is "in the world" (in other words, visible in the interface), it is easier to learn for the first time, but that efficiency "tends to be slowed up by the need to find and interpret external information." However, knowledge "in the head" (something that the user already knows how to do) "requires learning, which can be considerable," but "can be very efficient."

A good example of this can be seen by looking at the steps required to add an empty audio track in *Audacity* 1.3 for Windows and Apple *GarageBand* for iPad.

There is no indication in the Audacity interface on how to add a track. Right-clicking in the window does not create a contextual menu, and there are no buttons to add a new track in the toolbar. The user must explore the menus and find the "Tracks → Add New → Audio Track" menu item (see Figure 4.12). Once they find it, they know where it is. Furthermore, they can use the hotkey "Control + Shift + N" to add a new track very quickly. This is a very efficient way to add new tracks, but you have to know that it is there to take advantage of it. In other words, the knowledge has to be "in the head."

On the other hand, Apple *GarageBand* for iPad makes it very easy to learn how to add a new track. At the top of the interface, the "Instruments" button is prominently displayed. Pressing on this button brings you to a

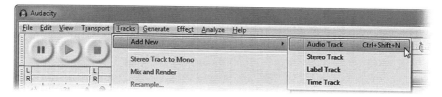

FIGURE 4.12   Adding a new audio track in Audacity. Audacity® software is copyright © 1999–2014 Audacity Team.

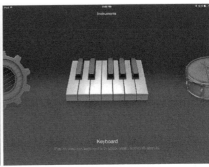

FIGURE 4.13 Adding a new audio track in the iPad version of Garage Band. © Apple.

list of instruments, with visual representations so you know what you are getting. From here, you can choose "Audio Recorder." You can then return to the tracks view to see your new track (see Figure 4.13). While this is easier to find because it is at the top of the interface and always visible—in other words, it is "in the world"—it requires more steps.

UNDERSTANDING THE MENTAL MODEL

Another important concept that helps us to understand how the users think is to understand their mental models and ensure that they match the conceptual model.

What Are the Mental Model and the Conceptual Model?

Susan Weinschenk, cognitive psychologist and author of several books on user experience, uses the following analogy to explain the difference between mental models and conceptual models.

A mental model is the way in which a user understands how something works. For example, almost everyone in the world has a mental model of a book: it contains pages, each page has words on it, and you can turn to the next page or the previous page.

By comparison, a conceptual model is the way in which an object or interface actually works. For example, imagine that you handed someone the device on top of the book in Figure 4.14. They have never seen this object before, and they have no idea what it is.

When they examine this device, they will notice that it has buttons and a screen. However, many other devices also have buttons and a screen: laptops, tablets, even calculators. What is this device? What does it do? It

FIGURE 4.14 Using the mental model of a book to accelerate the process of learning how to use an e-reader.

might take this person a while to figure out how it works, because they have no previous knowledge to draw on to help them understand how to use it.

Now imagine a different scenario where, before handing over the device, you tell them, "This is just like a book." As they examine the device, they compare their mental model of a book to the conceptual model of the device. They look at the words on the screen and think, "This must be like the pages on a book." They look at the buttons on both sides and think, "This must be for the next page and previous page." By referring to their mental model, they are able to make a connection to their existing mental model and understand what the device is—and how to use it—much more quickly and easily.

Major differences between the user's mental model and the tool's conceptual model is one of the key reasons why users have difficulty understanding how a tool works. Designing with the user's mental model in mind can have a big impact on improving the user experience of our game development tools.

Why Is It Important to Understand the User's Mental Model?

The mental models of programmers often include technical concepts that the user is not aware of, such as class structure and data models. Because these concepts come naturally to them, they might forget that the average user may not understand them. Consider the following terms: stereoscopy, rasterize, and Gouraud shading. These are all words that are part of the common vocabulary of graphics programmers. However, the majority of non-programmers may know these words as 3D imaging, pixel-based, and smooth shading. Even though these terms may not be

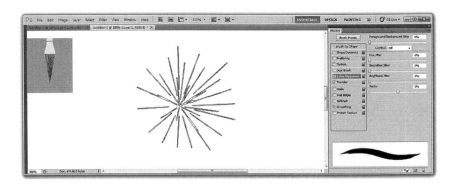

FIGURE 4.15 Adobe Photoshop uses the mental model of a paintbrush to make it easier to learn the settings in the Brush panel, reducing the amount of time spent in the think phase. Adobe product screenshot(s) reprinted with permission from Adobe Systems Incorporated.

perfectly accurate, they are often interchangeable and may be the most recognizable terms for the majority of users.

The brushes palette in Adobe Photoshop provides a good example of this (see Figure 4.15). There is plenty of technical terminology in the brushes palette. To create or modify a brush, you can set values for abstract sounding concepts such as "Roundness," "Angle Jitter," and "Purity." There are categories with names like "Shape Dynamics," "Transfer," and "Dual Brush." Even something with a simple name like "Spacing" can cause the user to ask, "The spacing of what? And, how much spacing do I want?"

A large proportion of the users many not think of brushes in those terms. There are accustomed to brushes in fine arts. They think about brushes visually, and how the brush will look when painting on a canvas. Fortunately, the bottom of the Brushes panel has a preview of what the brush will look like when it is used to create a curved stroke, and the upper left-hand corner of the windows shows the profile of the brush (see the top left and bottom right of Figure 4.15). This not only allows a beginner to simply adjust the numbers until they see the brushstroke they are looking for, but it also allows them to move closer to understanding what the numbers mean by immediately seeing the effect that each setting has on the brushstroke.

Another example is the Tree Creator in the Unity game engine. This tool represents the tree structure in a simple way that anyone can understand: it visualizes the trunk, branches, and leaves in a tree-like view (see Figure 4.16). It is possible that underneath, the tree is represented by a

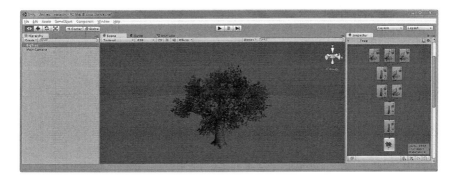

FIGURE 4.16   The Tree Creator in the Unity engine visualizes the structure of a tree in a way that matches the user's mental model, reducing the time spent in the think phase.

complex data model, but the user does not need to know that. This conceptual model is much closer to their mental model of the parts that make up a tree.

INTERVIEW STAKEHOLDERS

One of the first steps to improving the user experience of a tool is to interview the stakeholders. It is surprising how many people forget this fundamental step! Here are a few suggestions on what kinds of questions to ask the stakeholders.

How Do You Measure Success?

The first and probably most important question to ask is how the stakeholders measure success. Is it by making the tools more efficient, easier to learn, or some other measurement? This information is key to determining how you will measure the success of your efforts. It is normal for these to be more business-related as compared to the users' goals. These measurements of success are essentially the stakeholders' goals.

Who Are the Primary Users?

The stakeholders can also be helpful in giving you the names of people currently using the tool, so you can watch them work. If they cannot give you the names of primary users, they can probably give you the names of people who work with the primary users, such as their team leads and supervisors. This question is also important to ask because many problems in resource allocation can arise from the stakeholders being unaware of who the primary users are.

Linking Stakeholder Goals and User Goals

Once you have identified the stakeholder goals, you will want to try to find a connection between their goals and the user goals, to ensure that they can be connected. For example, imagine that one of the user goals is to optimize the level geometry to improve performance. At the same time, one of the stakeholder goals is to have the game run at 60 FPS. There is a clear connection between the two goals.

In contrast, imagine that another one of the stakeholder goals is to improve the efficiency of a tool used for creating a gritty, urban environment with minimal impact on texture memory. Meanwhile, one of the user goals is to have an easy-to-learn tool that generates hyper-realistic trees with high-resolution textures.

When one or more user goals have no connection to any of the stakeholder goals, this could be a sign that tools development resources will not be invested correctly, leading to potential problems.

PERFORM CONTEXTUAL ANALYSES

Once we have a list of users of the tool, we can watch them work using a technique called *contextual analysis*. The word *contextual* emphasizes the fact that we want to watch the user working in the context of their environment, as opposed to an interview, which could take place anywhere. In other words, we want to watch them working at their desk, with their tools, as they normally do. This ensures that we get a sense of what it is really like when they use the tool.

How to Perform a Contextual Analysis

To perform a contextual analysis, start by making a list of the users to meet and booking individual meetings with them. When you sit down with a user to watch them work, keep the following questions and ideas in mind.*

Introduction

Some users might be uncomfortable with someone showing up at their desk and asking questions. Remember to take the time to introduce yourself, and ask the user about themselves. Ask them how long they have been doing their job, or ask them about their favorite game. If they have action

---

* For an in-depth approach to doing interviews and performing contextual analyses, you can also read Steve Portigal's book *Interviewing Users*.

figures or toys on their desk, ask about them. Even if you know the user, questions such as these help to ease into the contextual analysis.

It is also very common for people to believe that they are being judged on their performance, or that this is part of their yearly review. If this is the case, remind them that not only is it safe to make mistakes, but that making mistakes might help to find and fix problems with the tool. Emphasize that the tool is being evaluated, not them.

All of these things help to break the ice, which will result in the user being more likely to tell you how they really feel, instead of what they think you want to hear.

Ask about Goals

After the introduction, ask the user why they use a certain tool or how a tool fits into their pipeline, and what they are trying to accomplish with it. This will help to understand what their goals are. For example, a user does not think, "I want to use the mesh exporter"; they think, "I want to add a new object to the game engine." That is their true goal. Focus on understanding what their goals are when they are using a tool. Ask why several times if it helps to get to the root of the goal.

Master and Apprentice

Even if you know the tools that the users are using, imagine that you are the apprentice and that they are the master. Ask them to show you how to use the tool from their perspective. Ask them questions, and spend as much time as you can just listening. This will give you a better idea of how they use the tools, which can help you identify how to make them better.

Re-Direct Feature Talk to Goal Talk

If issues with specific features start to dominate the contextual analysis, try to re-direct the discussion back to goals. For example, if the user starts to describe how to change a feature, respond with, "How would that help you accomplish your goal?"

Don't Ask Leading Questions

It is important not to ask questions that could force the user into thinking that they must answer one way or the other. Questions like "Do you think that this should be red?" lead the user to believe that there is a right or wrong answer. Instead, ask an open question such as "In your opinion, what color would mean danger or error?"

Ask the User to Talk Out Loud

As the user is performing their task, ask them to talk out loud about what they are thinking. Users can get wrapped up in what they are doing and forget to do this. If this happens, gently remind the user by saying, "So what are you thinking right now?" or "What's going through your mind at this point?" Some users will be uncomfortable with talking out loud, so use common sense to determine how you need them to do this.

Resist the Urge to Help

It might be difficult, but it is very important to resist helping the user during the contextual analysis. They might have difficulty with a task, or they might say something about the tool that you know is wrong. If you correct them, or interrupt them and tell them what to do, you may miss valuable information that could explain why they are having trouble. That information can help you find a way to make the tool better.

After the contextual analysis is over, you may choose to tell the user how to do the task, or correct their understanding of a certain concept.

Start Wide, Then Focus Down

If you are working on a massive, monolithic tool, remember: even the biggest content creation tool is made up of parts. For example, a fully featured level editor looks big, but it is essentially made up of a collection of smaller tools that communicate with each other. If the amount of work is overwhelming, try to start wide with the first few contextual analyses, and then focus down to a smaller part that you feel will give the biggest return on investment.

Team of Two

It is also strongly recommended that you perform the contextual analysis with two people. This has a dual purpose: The first is that asking questions, watching the user, and taking notes all at once is very difficult. The second is that a contextual inquiry is a great opportunity to invite someone who might not have the chance to watch the users work, such as a stakeholder, or another developer. This can help to get buy-in from everyone involved.

What Can We Do after the Contextual Analyses?

When you are satisfied with the amount of information that you have gathered through contextual analyses, go through your notes and make a prioritized list of the most common goals shared by the most frequent users. If you end up with more than a dozen goals, then you are probably trying to do too much at once, or you are including goals that are edge cases. Either concentrate on a smaller part of the tool, or reevaluate who your target users are.

These goals can be used as a starting point to create task flows, mental models, personas, scenario storyboards, and most importantly, measurements. Each of these techniques is described below.

CREATE TASK FLOWS

When attempting to accomplish a goal, a user may execute one or more tasks. Each task is made up of a series of actions. Task flows are a way of thinking about the flow of those actions, which can help everyone involved in the development of the tool to have a shared vision of how the actions are connected. This makes it easier to pinpoint where improvement is needed.

How to Create a Task Flow

A task flow is essentially a flowchart that represents how the user performs a task, with each node representing an action. For each action that the users perform, make a node. Connect it to the other actions to create a flow. If the user branches off, split off a node and continue from there (see Figure 4.17).

You can create a task flow for each user and then merge them into one task flow that represents the average. In the case that a significant number of users perform different actions, note the percentage of users who typically execute one action as opposed to the other, as well as the frequency at which they perform that action. This will allow you to identify which part of the task flow represents the majority of the users' time, which can help you to prioritize what to work on first.

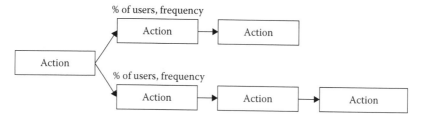

FIGURE 4.17   The structure of a task flow.

From the User's Perspective

Keep in mind that a task flow is done from the user's perspective. As a result, the task flow should not include technical details that the users do not understand. To help reinforce this, the text in each node should contain a verb describing the action, such as "select the object" or "export to the engine," instead of "fire a ray-cast" or "server parses XAML data."

Adding Details

During the contextual analysis, you may have taken note of where the user had problems or made mistakes. You can note where these issues occur in the task flow. For each issue, also consider the following:

- Is this an efficiency problem? If so, which part of the action cycle could be the problem: the look, think, or act? Is it more than one?

- Is this a learnability problem? Will making the feature easier to learn result in it being less efficient? Is that a problem, considering how frequently the feature is used?

Creating an Optimized Task Flow

In addition to creating a task flow that represents the average, it could also be useful to create an optimal task flow. To do this, you could ask, "Which actions could be removed? Which actions could take less time? Which actions are difficult for new users to understand?" You could then create a new task flow that represents the optimal situation. This can be a great way to set clear objectives for everyone involved in the development of the tool.

DISCOVER THE USERS' MENTAL MODEL

During the contextual analysis, you can also take some time to understand the mental model of the users. A few techniques can be used to do this. These can be used with several users, and then the results can be combined to create an average mental model of the users that can be shared with everyone involved in the development of the tool.

Card Sort

This technique is useful when we do not know how the user organizes different terms or concepts in their mind. For example, let us assume that we are building a tool that contains a list of objects that we can place in a level.

We can place many different types of objects: enemies, weapons, power-ups, lights, particle effects, and trigger boxes. In the mind of a developer, lights and enemies are related because they are derived from the same class that represents the position of an object. For this reason, it might seem logical to group them together. However, in the user's mental model, lights have more to do with trigger boxes and particle effects, because they are used together to create the lighting and ambience of the level. The users do not associate lights and enemies, even though they are related in the code.

Here is how a card sort can be used to do this:

1. Write each term or concept on a card.

2. Give the cards to a user and ask them to lay them out on a table in groups that make sense to them (see Figure 4.18).

3. When they are done, ask them why they organized the cards the way that they did.

4. Finally, take a photo or write down how all the cards were organized, and take note of the user's name so you can ask follow-up questions later.

5. Repeat steps 2 through 4 with a new user. Do this with as many users as you can.

FIGURE 4.18   Example of a card sort.

Once you are done, compare the results across all users to find trends and common groupings. You can use a spreadsheet to do this, or you can use web-based tools to facilitate the process.*

User Objects

The term *user object* describes the mental model of a specific type of object that the user can manipulate. The word *user* in *user object* is important here, since this is about how the user sees it, not how it is coded. For example, the class definition for an entity in a level editor may define rotation in radians with an angle-axis Vector4. However, the user may not know what any of those words mean, and they simply think of rotation as being between 0 and 360 degrees, on the x-, y-, and z-axes.

For each user object, we take note of how the user perceives them by making a list of attributes and actions: the attributes of the object, and the actions that you perform with the object. If the discussion about the user objects turns to features requests, steer the conversation back to what the user's goals are, and how they can be translated into attributes and actions.

Once we have performed a contextual analysis with a few users, we can start to identify the most common attributes and actions requested by most users. This will help us to focus on the right features used by the majority of users.

For example, if we worked with a user to create a user object for a point light, the results might look like Figure 4.19. This user's mental model of a point light is that it has the attributes of color, intensity, and range. They also consider the color as being set as HSV (hue, saturation, and value), the intensity as a number (where 100 is equal to 100 percent intensity), and the range is measured in meters.

Object	Attributes	Actions
Point light	Color (HSV) Intensity (100 = 100%) Range (in meters)	Move light Change the color Set the intensity Set range Enable or disable

FIGURE 4.19   Example of a user object for a point light.

---

* Two popular options are Optimal Sort (http://www.optimalworkshop.com/optimalsort.htm) and Websort (http://dirtarchitecture.wordpress.com/websort/). These services also provide an automated analysis such as most common groupings, trends, and so on.

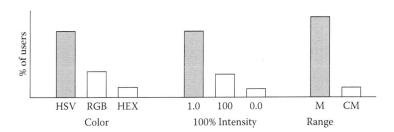

FIGURE 4.20 Choosing how data is represented based upon the most common attributes of the user objects.

If you have a large number of users, you could add up the results of the user objects to determine the most common attributes and actions, in an effort to build a shared mental model for point lights (see shaded bars in Figure 4.20).

Note that the user who created the point light user object earlier preferred 100 percent intensity to be the number 100, whereas the majority of users preferred 1.0. Remember that we are not going to make everyone happy. Start with 1.0. If it becomes a problem to a significant number of users, we can always add an option to switch between 1.0 and 100.

Developers who are familiar with object-oriented programming will notice that—although they are from the user's perspective—creating user objects is almost like describing a class. Therefore, doing this exercise before writing code can accelerate developer productivity, because it provides a starting point that provides the functionality that the users are expecting.

ESTABLISH MEASUREMENTS

One of the most important aspects of the User-Centered Design process is measuring progress, which helps to ensure that you are going in the right direction. The process described in Jeff Gothelf's book *Lean UX* focuses on doing small, rapid iterations and measuring Key Performance Indicators, or KPIs. The ISO 9241-210 specification provides examples about what to measure, and how. Taking the time to track these measurements is one of the best ways to ensure that your efforts are improving the user experience.

In Chapter 1, we learned that there are many different ways to measure usability, and that this book focuses on efficiency and learnability. Choosing what to measure depends on a variety of factors, such as the goals of the users and the stakeholders, as well as the experience level of the users.

Measuring Efficiency

If the goals of the stakeholders are related to producing assets faster with fewer people or more assets with the same number of people, efficiency could be the right choice. During the contextual inquiry, if a large proportion of the users complain that the tool is slow, or that the number of steps required to complete specific tasks is too high, this could also point to the decision to measure efficiency.

Furthermore, if the users are mostly experts who are accustomed to complex tools, and they have a deadline looming on the horizon, this could further confirm a decision to measure efficiency. This decision could mean that the users are required to receive some training on the changes to the interface, and they may require documentation. However, the intention would be higher efficiency overall.

To measure efficiency within the task flow, you can use a stopwatch to time how long the user takes to perform either each task or specific actions. Ensure that the users are working with the same assets or values, if possible, so that the numbers are comparable. These numbers can be averaged across multiple users to get a baseline measurement that you can compare against each time you go through the Analysis phase. We will talk more about this in Chapters 6 and 7.

You may also be able to measure efficiency of tasks and actions by using metrics. However, it can be challenging to make decisions based only on these numbers, because it may not be possible to determine if the task was completed successfully, and because the user could be away from their desk in the middle of an action, inflating the results. As always, a combination of metrics and watching the users work can give the best results.

Measuring Learnability

If the goals of the stakeholders are to ramp up new users faster, or to reduce support costs (such as the salaries of people writing the documentation or the time spent by expert users training users and answering their questions), learnability may be a better measurement. Additionally, if you notice that during the contextual inquiry the users have difficulty remembering all of the various functions within a tool, or they make many mistakes that could potentially be avoided by understanding how the tool works, this could confirm a decision to measure learnability.

In addition, if the content creators are less experienced, and the team is still ramping up to full production mode, leaning more toward learnability could be a better choice. Keep in mind that a focus on improving learnability could have an adverse effect on efficiency, and the intention is to compensate for that by making the tools easier to learn.

As we discovered earlier in the chapter, a tool is considered to have good learnability if a new user unfamiliar with the tool can accomplish a task on the first attempt. This can be measured by using a stopwatch to time how long it takes the user to complete a task successfully, with specific assets or values.

Measuring Both

Finally, it is possible to design a tool where the majority of the features are both easy to learn and efficient to use. This often takes much longer to measure and design compared to simply choosing one or the other, because efficiency and learnability can sometimes be in opposition with each other. As a result, you may have to compromise, or choose to improve both for only the most frequently used features in your tool.

There is a good reason why very few tools are both efficient and learnable: finding a balance between the two is one of the biggest challenges in user experience design.

ADVANCED TECHNIQUES

Personas

If you perform a contextual analysis on a large number of users and it is difficult to communicate the goals and mental models for all of those users, you have the option of creating personas. Personas are archetypes of people who represent the majority of the people that use the tool. Not only does it make it easier for you to see the big picture of whom you are building for, but it also helps to communicate who these people are.

How to Create Personas

Here is a very basic approach to creating a persona: study your contextual analysis notes and try to identify the most common goals and mental models. Group related goals and mental models together. Each group will become a persona. You may choose to create a separate persona per job role, such as one for level designers and one for animators, or be more specific, such as separate personas for AI programmers and physics programmers.[*]

---

[*] For more on creating personas, you can read Chapter 5 of Cooper, Reinmann, and Cronin's book *About Face 3*, or Adlin and Pruitt's *The Essential Persona Lifecycle*.

Goals
Nullam quis
Dapibus augue
Vitae blandit justo
Donec malesuad

Mental Models
Ellentesque ornare
Tincidunt felis
At ultrices aliquam

Patrick
Level Designer

Goals
Morbi metus sapien
Blandit eget
Ullamcorper tinci

Mental Models
Pellentesque quis
Nibh in dignissim
Elit sapien maecena
Fasellus imperdiet

Rochelle
Animator

FIGURE 4.21   Example personas.

It is also important to give each persona a realistic name and a natural-looking picture. For example, giving a persona the name "Moe the Modeler" and using a cartoon character as a photo will result in people not taking the personas seriously.*

Personas created to represent users of a game development tool might look something like Figure 4.21.

Scenario Storyboards

To create an even deeper understanding of context, you can also choose to create scenario storyboards. Scenario storyboards resemble the storyboards we use when planning a game cinematic (see Figure 4.22). The

FIGURE 4.22   Example scenario storyboard.

---

* You can auto-generate realistic names and pictures from websites like http://www.randomuser.
me, or you can use a more complete persona creation solution with tools such as http://www.
usabilitytools.com/features-benefits/persona-creator.

purpose of a scenario is to explore how the tool is used in a variety of contexts. They are very useful for ensuring that everyone involved in the development of the tool understands and agrees on how the tool is supposed to be used.

How to Create Scenario Storyboards

To create a scenario storyboard, first choose one or more user goals or tasks. If you have also created personas, you can choose to feature them in the scenario storyboard. Each frame in the storyboard depicts an action performed by the personas while they are using the tool, and it ends in the successful completion of their task or goals.*

Scenario storyboards do not include references to the user interface. Instead, they show how the personas would interact with the user objects. This keeps the scenario storyboards at a high level so that they do not influence us into assuming that the interface must function or look a certain way. This enables us to focus on finding the best possible design solution to achieve the users' goals.

The quality of the drawings is not important. However, if you need some assistance producing storyboards, many web-based tools are available.†

WRAPPING UP

In this chapter, we learned about the Analysis phase of the User-Centered Design process. We discussed the value of watching users work, the limitations of metrics and focus groups, and the importance of thinking in terms of the problems that we are trying to solve (not the features we want to implement). We also learned about human–computer interaction, the action cycle, its effects on efficiency and learnability, as well as the concept of the user's mental model. Finally, we learned a variety of techniques to be used during the Analysis phase, such as interviewing stakeholders, performing contextual analyses, creating task flows, and establishing measurements.

In the next chapter, we will discuss concepts and techniques to be used during the Design phase of the User-Centered Design process.

---

* For more on creating scenarios, you can also read Chapter 6 of Cooper, Reinmann, and Cronin's book *About Face 3*.
† Storyboard That (http://www.storyboardthat.com/) and Amazon Storyteller (http://studios.amazon.com/storyteller) are two popular examples.

CHAPTER 5

Design

WHAT WILL WE LEARN IN THIS CHAPTER?

Concepts

- Understanding how the eyes and the brain work together

- How a visual language can help humans and computers communicate

- The importance of using interaction patterns

Techniques

- How hierarchy can guide the user through the interface

- Making the interface easier to understand with natural mapping

- How to use representation to help the user work with and understand complex data

- How to use feedback to let the user know what the tool is doing

- Using feed-forward to help the user learn what an action will do, before they commit to it

- How to use grouping to associate information in a way that the users expect

- How to use chunking to make it easier for the user to process more information at once

- How to use excise to make the user work faster (or slower, if necessary)

- Using progressive disclosure to design an interface that is simple for beginners and powerful for experts

HOW THE BRAIN AND THE EYES WORK TOGETHER

Previous generations of the Sony PlayStation have included unique microprocessors, such as the Emotion Engine and the Cell. Getting the best performance out of these chips required specialized knowledge and programming skills. Each chip had its own quirks and idiosyncrasies. Expecting a programmer to get the best performance out of these chips without first understanding their architecture would be unrealistic.

Designing tools for people is no different. The brain is a microprocessor in its own right and has strengths and weaknesses. Just as understanding the architecture of a chip allows us to be better console developers, understanding how the brain works can help us design tools with a better user experience.

Our Brains Decide What We See

As tools developers, we may have had the experience of adding a new button to an interface, only to realize that very few users notice it. All the work that was put into the feature is lost since no one knows that it is there. You may have asked yourself, "Why don't the users see that button?"

It may come as a surprise to learn that we do not always see what we think we do. Our brain fills in the blanks. A great example of this is our blind spot. On the inside of our eye are rods and cones, responsible for detecting colors and contrast. However, at the point where the optic nerve connects to the eyeball, there are no rods and cones. As a result, we cannot see in that spot.

To test this, hold this book away from your face and cover your left eye. Now, look at the cross in Figure 5.1. Slowly move the book closer to your face until the dot disappears. Where did the dot go? The answer is that your eye does not have any rods or cones where the circle should be, so your brain fills in the missing information.

After experiencing this, you can begin to understand how it is possible that users do not see the new button that you added.

FIGURE 5.1   Testing your blind spot.

FIGURE 5.2   Examples of how our brains are optimized to interpret specific patterns.

Our Brains Are Optimized for Specific Patterns

Figure 5.2 contains a series of shapes. Most people see a triangle on the left, even though there is no triangle, only three pies. In the middle, we recognize the shape as a circle, even though the line is broken. Finally, on the right, our eye is immediately attracted to the cross that looks different.[*]

Our brains are hardwired to interpret these specific visual patterns very quickly, which is probably a result of natural selection. Consider the image in the middle of Figure 5.2: if the circle is a saber-toothed tiger and the missing parts are trees that it is hiding behind, the ability to recognize the shape—despite the missing parts—may have kept our ancestors alive.

VISUAL LANGUAGE

It turns out that if we want to understand visual language, video games provide some of the best examples. The visual language for a game is made of multiple elements, and two of the most important are shape and color.

At GDC 2008, Valve's Jason Mitchell presented a talk[†] about the distinct visual language of *Team Fortress 2*. As the game is a multiplayer first-person shooter, identifying the class of the enemy you are fighting from far away is very important, and so each class has a unique shape, or silhouette (see the top of Figure 5.3). Finding the enemy base is also extremely important, and so each team's base has a distinctive architectural style: warm colors and angular shapes for the RED team versus cool colors and orthogonal shapes for the BLU team (see the bottom of Figure 5.3). Once you learn this language, you can see which class of enemies you are facing and which base you are in, at a glance.

---

[*] These are all examples from Gestalt psychology, which you can read more about here: http://en.wikipedia.org/wiki/Gestalt_psychology.

[†] You can see the entire presentation here: http://www.valvesoftware.com/publications/2008/GDC2008_StylizationWithAPurpose_TF2.pdf.

FIGURE 5.3 The visual language of *Team Fortress 2.* © Valve Corporation.

Learning the Language

As the gamer learns how to communicate with the visual language, it becomes a conversation: the screen shows the status of the game, and the gamer responds with the controller. The gamer may also learn the language faster if the same elements are seen in other games of the same genre. For example, in the vast majority of first-person shooter games, when we see an arrow shape that is colored red on the edge of the screen, we know that someone is attacking us from that angle, and we instinctively respond to the threat with the controller.

The same can be said for game development tools. If we use familiar and consistent shapes and colors, the user spends less time learning the tool, and they will know what to do at a glance.

Familiar Icons

Some people believe that the save icon is outdated and should be replaced. The typical save icon represents a 3.5″ diskette, which most people have not used to save a file since the 1990s (see the left side of Figure 5.4). Recently,

FIGURE 5.4 Familiar icons are recognized and interpreted more quickly than new designs or "ideal" representations.

some of the best designers in the world tried to design a replacement but were unable to reach a consensus.* Despite being out of date, the save icon prevails for one important reason: because our brains are better at recognizing a familiar shape than interpreting a new one, even if it is a more appropriate representation.

Consider the iconography for "call" on a smartphone or "train crossing" on a street sign (see the middle and right side of Figure 5.4, respectively). We do not see rotary telephone receivers or steam engines very often these days, yet their silhouettes are iconic—pardon the pun—and continue to be used because they are the most familiar shapes for those concepts.

When choosing icons for your game development tools, strive for familiarity over a new design. Although the shape of an icon may seem out of date, it is more important that the user can recognize it as opposed to having the perfect representation.

Color Consistency

Users of Microsoft Visual Studio—or any other modern IDE—are accustomed to the concept of color syntax: specific keywords use the same color consistently, making it easy to pick out variables, functions, and comments. There is no denying that using color to communicate in this way is an extremely useful tool: for example, color makes it easier to fix an unterminated string. While we should take advantage of using color to communicate with the user, we need to ensure that our tools use color consistently, and that the colors match existing standards.

For example, imagine if Visual Studio had inconsistent color syntax. In some cases, variables would be blue, and in other cases, they would be green. This would frustrate any programmer. However, many game development tools do not use color consistently. In one window, an object may be purple, while in another window, it may be orange.

In Microsoft Excel, when the value of a cell is negative, it is colored red to indicate a problem. This is because accountants want to see where money is being lost. However, imagine if that color was green. All around the world, the colors green, yellow, and red in software interfaces are accepted to represent OK, caution, and danger,† so a problem represented by the color green would seem unnatural. Unfortunately, some game

---

* You can see that discussion here: http://branch.com/b/redesigning-the-save-symbol-let-s-do-this.
† These standards were originally recommended by the Vienna Convention on Road Signs and Signals. Read more here: http://en.wikipedia.org/wiki/Convention_on_Road_Signs_and_Signals.

More contrast   Less contrast

FIGURE 5.5   Our eyes are able to read text with stronger contrast more quickly and accurately.

development tools use bright red in situations where there is no problem, leading to confusion and concern among the users.

To design an interface with a better user experience, pick colors that are consistent and match existing standards.*

Legible Contrast

Although our brain works hard to compensate for the limitations of our eyes, there are some things that it simply cannot do. To ensure that the user is able to see the visual language that we have designed, we must also consider the ability of our eyes to see contrast.

When the shade for text and the background are too close to each other, our eyes have difficulty making out the shapes (see the right side of Figure 5.5). Fortunately, there are standards for contrast that we can follow and tools we can use to ensure maximum legibility.†

A Note on Dark Interfaces

The popularity of dark interfaces has increased in the last few years, especially in the case of content creation tools. One of the first tools to adopt a dark interface was Autodesk Combustion. Other content creation tools started including a "dark mode," such as Adobe Photoshop and Autodesk 3ds max. When Apple announced a dark mode for OSX Yosemite at WWDC 2014, it prompted cheers from the crowd. Now, dark interfaces can even be found in tools that are not used exclusively by artists, such as Unity and Microsoft Visual Studio.

The fact is that our eyes have more difficulty seeing contrast when light text is used on a dark background. To experience this effect, try using a tool with an interface that can be switched between dark and light on a laptop outside on a sunny day, such as one of the many tools in the Adobe suite, or the Unity game engine. When you switch between the dark and light interfaces, you will notice that you can see more details on the light interface.

---

* Microsoft's recommendations for color can be found here: http://msdn.microsoft.com/en-us/library/windows/desktop/dn742482.asp.
† Here is a list if tools from the W3C website to verify that contrast standards are being respected: http://www.w3.org/TR/UNDERSTANDING-WCAG20/visual-audio-contrast-contrast.html#visual-audio-contrast-contrast-resources-head.

However, this should not lead us to conclude that light interfaces are better. To do this would be to forget the importance of watching users work. We need to understand context in which the dark interface was developed in the first place: Combustion is a tool for film compositing, typically used in a dark editing room with no windows. The users found that a lighter interface blinded them, and that a darker interface was more comfortable, given the context: working in dark editing room with no windows.

The point is that light and dark interfaces each have their place, and the best choice depends on the context of the environment of the users. When in doubt, give the users a choice of one or the other.

INTERACTION PATTERNS

One of the first professions to understand the significance of humans interacting with patterns was architecture.* Through our life experience, we have learned that a series of stacked cubes is a flight of stairs that can be climbed, and a rectangle with a handle is a door that can be opened. Just like a visual language, when we see these shapes, our brain recognizes the pattern and we know what to do.

The same goes for user interfaces. For example, through experience, we have learned the difference between radio buttons and checkboxes: one lets the user choose only one option at a time, while the other lets the user choose more than one option at once (see Figure 5.6). When we see them, we know how they are supposed to work instantly.

It may be tempting to create new and unique user interface elements or behaviors for existing controls. This might be because we feel that we know a better way for the user to manipulate the data, or it looks like an interesting challenge. We must do our best to resist this temptation. Not only could it result in decreased learnability and efficiency, but it will also take more time to create and maintain the code for a control that does not already exist.

FIGURE 5.6 The importance of following interaction guidelines and patterns: the majority of users have learned how a radio button works (left), and how it is different from a checkbox (right).

---

* The book *A Pattern Language* by Alexander, Ishikawa, Silverstein, et al. is generally regarded as one of the best books on the patterns of architecture and urban design.

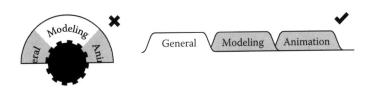

FIGURE 5.7 Changing the current view: a non-standard pattern (left) compared to a standard pattern (right).

For example, if your tool requires a control to switch between different views, it might be appealing to develop a dial that the user can turn to set the current view. While it is true that using a dial to switch between views is more common for physical devices, a more standardized pattern for a desktop software-based content creation tool would be tabs (see Figure 5.7). They are common in software user interfaces, and most users are familiar with them.*

What Happens When We Do Not Follow Guidelines?

While it is true that there are rare times where the advantages of a new pattern outweigh the disadvantages, we should strive for familiarity as much as possible. This means following existing interaction patterns guidelines, such as those created and maintained by Microsoft and Apple.

Imagine that we introduce a new interaction pattern to our tool. This pattern is unfamiliar to all of the users and must be learned. When the user sees the pattern, they spend more time in the think and look phases of the action cycle. If the new pattern does not improve the efficiency of the tool, this means that the new pattern has actually made the usability of our tool worse!

Established interaction patterns do not have to be learned. We know how they work from experience. They have been streamlined over time. If used correctly, users will learn the tool faster (because they are familiar with the interface) and be more efficient (because they can jump back and forth between different tools without having to adjust the way they work).

Who Establishes Interaction Patterns?

An interaction pattern becomes a standard because it works well. Just as our brain's ability to see visual patterns evolved to keep us from being

---

* This is also dependent on the platform. For example, to toggle a value on and off, a switch control is more common in tablets and smartphones, while a checkbox is more common in desktop software applications.

eaten by a saber-toothed tiger, interaction patterns survive because they have proven to be some of the most effective and well-established solutions to a given problem within a specific context.

It is unusual for new interaction patterns to be established by anyone other than big companies such as Apple, Microsoft, and Adobe.[*] Because they have such a large market share, many people are exposed to their products and become familiar with their interaction patterns.[†]

There are times when Apple, Adobe, and Microsoft deviate slightly from their own guidelines. However, the vast majority of their applications follow the guidelines and use the same patterns consistently. We should do the same. If the interaction patterns are standardized, users can focus on creating content, instead of learning how to use the interface.

How to Choose the Right Interaction Pattern

If you have read the books *Design Patterns: Elements of Reusable Object-Oriented Software* by Gamma, Helm, Johnson, and Vlissides or *Code Complete* by Steve McConnell, you know that design patterns are a solution to a problem within a given context. Many interaction pattern libraries also use this format to help you decide which one is best to use.

For example, when the problem is choosing one unique option from a list, and the context is that there are between two and seven options, the Microsoft guidelines suggest using radio buttons. However, in the context that there are more than seven options and not a lot of space to display them, a drop-down is suggested.[‡] (See Figure 5.8.)

Many guidelines derive from this format to help you choose the right interaction pattern. When in doubt, implement it and watch the users work with it.

---

[*] The guidelines for Microsoft Windows and Apple OSX can be found below. To the best of my knowledge, the design guidelines for Adobe products are not publicly available.
   http://msdn.microsoft.com/library/windows/desktop/dn688964.aspx
   https://developer.apple.com/library/mac/documentation/UserExperience/Conceptual/AppleHIGuidelines/Intro/Intro.html

[†] In some ways, Apple's keynote presentations—watched by millions of people all over the world—are a training session on how to use their products. This can have a huge impact on the perception of how easy to learn their products are!

[‡] See the guidelines on radio buttons here: http://msdn.microsoft.com/en-us/library/windows/desktop/dn742436%28v=vs.85%29.aspx.

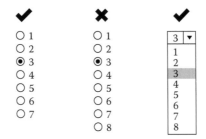

FIGURE 5.8   An example of how guidelines help to determine when to use radio buttons versus a drop-down menu.

What to Do if a Pattern Does Not Exist in the Guidelines

There may be times when the user interface control that you need does not exist in the Microsoft or Apple guidelines. In this case, the next best thing to do is to find as many examples of other similar controls in other software, and look for similarities in the look and functionality.

For example, Microsoft and Apple may not have guidelines for a control that resizes a two-dimensional object. However, if you compare almost any image manipulation software (especially those made by Adobe), you will see that a rectangle around one or more selected objects, with handles at the four corners that you can drag to resize, is a common pattern that will be familiar to most users.

HIERARCHY

In the world of graphic design, hierarchy can be used to draw the user's attention to a specific part of the interface. This can be useful if you must show a lot of information in your interface, but you want the user to focus on a specific part that will help them to accomplish their goals.

How Can Hierarchy Improve Usability?

Efficiency

By using hierarchy, we can influence the user's gaze. This can reduce the amount of time spent in the look phase of the action cycle while the user is scanning the interface to find what they are looking for.

Learnability

We can use hierarchy to attract the user's eye to specific parts of the interface, making it easier for beginners to find the basic functions they are looking for when seeing the tool for the first time.

```
P  PPP      TTTT      SSSS      CCCC
    PPP      TTTT       SS      CCCC
PPPPP      TTTT      Sss      CCCC
PPPPP      TTTT      SSSS      CCCC
```

FIGURE 5.9   Example of hierarchy, from left to right: position, thickness, size, and contrast.

Understanding Hierarchy

Like a visual language, hierarchy uses shape and color to influence where the user looks. Hierarchy is defined by four properties: position, thickness, size, and contrast (see Figure 5.9, from left to right).

Position
Objects that are placed close to each other are considered grouped. This also means that objects with a lot of white space around them will stand out, attracting the user's attention first relative to the other objects.

Thickness
Thicker objects are often seen as having more importance and will typically be noticed before thinner objects. A good example of this is bold text versus regular text.

Size
A single object that is a different size compared to the other objects around it is likely to be noticed first. The fine print in an advertisement is a good example of this. The advertisers want you to notice the text in the ad first, not the fine print!

Contrast
We tend to notice objects that have more contrast first and then other objects with less contrast after. In fact, newborn babies see extreme contrast before they can see subtle contrast, which is why many baby toys have highly contrasted shapes and colors.

What Are Examples of Patterns That Use Hierarchy?
The Google weather card is an excellent example of hierarchy (see Figure 5.10). If the user's goal is to see the current temperature, the design is very efficient at using all four elements of hierarchy to draw the user's

FIGURE 5.10 The Google Weather card uses hierarchy to help the user focus on the most important information first. Google and the Google logo are registered trademarks of Google Inc., used with permission.

attention to that information. The current temperature is by itself, surrounded by white space (position), it is bigger and bolder than the other text (size and thickness), and it is 100 percent black on 100 percent white (contrast). All of these properties in combination influence our eyes to look at the current temperature first and then scan the rest of the interface after.

As you can see in Figure 5.11, new e-mails in Gmail feature two properties of hierarchy: they are bold (thickness) and are written in black text on

📭 Primary	😃 Social	🏷 Promotions	+
☐ ☆ **Gmail Team**	Stay more organized with Gmail's inbox -		6:55 am
☐ ☆ **Gmail Team**	**The best of Gmail, wherever you are**		6:55 am
☐ ☆ **Gmail Team**	Three tips to get the most out of Gmail -		6:55 am

FIGURE 5.11 The Gmail inbox uses hierarchy to make unread messages stand out. Google and the Google logo are registered trademarks of Google Inc., used with permission.

a white background (contrast). By comparison, read e-mails are not bold and are written in black text on a gray background. All of this draws your eye to the new e-mails.

CONSTRAINTS

Constraints impose limits on what the user can do. Their purpose is to protect the user from making mistakes, allowing them to focus on their work without having to worry about the limitations.

How Can Constraints Improve Usability?
Efficiency
Without constraints, the user may try to do something that will result in an error. Because of this, they will spend a lot of time in the think phase trying to understand why something is not working. Furthermore, limiting the user's choices means they spend less time in the look phase considering options that are not allowed anyway.

Learnability
Limiting the user's options also means that they have less to learn. The constraints make it clear what can and cannot be done.

Understanding Constraints
When we are deeply involved in the creation of a tool, we sometimes forget that not all users are aware of the system's technical limitations. Users will try things that we never thought possible.

When users make mistakes, not only does it affect their efficiency, but it can also make them feel frustrated and hesitant to explore the rest of the tool. Furthermore, constraints can protect bad assets from being shared with the rest of the production team—which affects everyone's productivity. Good constraints make the users more confident about using the tool, so they can focus on creating content.

What Are Good Constraints?
Some constraints have the best intentions to protect the user but still allow them to make mistakes. For example, USB cables use a small piece of plastic to prevent the user from plugging it in the wrong way (see the left side of Figure 5.12). However, this merely acts as a guide, and it is not guaranteed to work. As you may have experienced, sometimes it takes multiple attempts of plugging and flipping to insert a USB cable properly.

FIGURE 5.12 The USB cable and Lightning cable demonstrate different types of constraints.

There are other examples like this, such as jumper cables or component cables: the color code might seem like it protects the user, but mistakes are still possible.

One of the best examples of a cable that truly protects the user from making a mistake is the Apple Lightning cable (see the right side of Figure 5.12). Unlike the USB cable design, there is no wrong way to plug it in. You plug it in whichever way you want. Even better, the edges are rounded, helping to guide the plug into the charging port. Constraints that protect the user without having to think make for a better user experience.

What Are Examples of Patterns That Use Constraints?

A very basic constraint could be the use of a slider instead of a numeric input box when the value has a minimum and maximum value (see Figure 5.13). By adding a slider, it is impossible for the user to enter an incorrect value. Furthermore, the slider is a familiar interaction pattern, and users expect it to limit the range of values that can be entered,* as opposed to a numeric input box that sometimes rejects or readjusts the value.

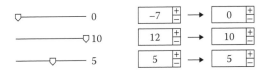

FIGURE 5.13 Sliders have clear constraints (left), as opposed to numeric input boxes with minimum and maximum values (right).

---

* You can refer to Microsoft's guidelines on sliders here: http://msdn.microsoft.com/en-us/library/windows/desktop/bb226811%28v=vs.85%29.aspx.

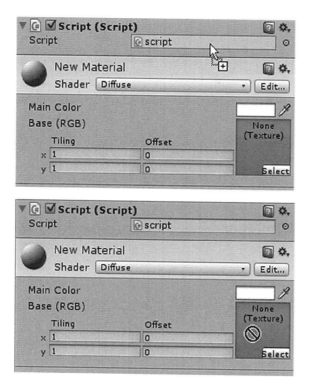

FIGURE 5.14   The Inspector in the Unity Engine uses constraints to ensure that a script can only be added where it is allowed.

Another example of constraints: limiting where an object can be dragged and dropped. For example, in the Unity game engine, you can only drag and drop a script on the Script input of a Game Object (see the top of Figure 5.14). This makes it impossible for a user to insert a script file in the wrong place, such as a texture map input (see the bottom of Figure 5.14).*

NATURAL MAPPING

An interface with good natural mapping means that the placement of the controls matches the actions that they perform. For example, buttons to move objects left and right are placed to the left and right of each other, instead of top and bottom.

---

* You can find guidelines for drag and drop in OSX here: https://developer.apple.com/library/ mac/documentation/userexperience/conceptual/applehiguidelines/TechnologyGuidelines/ TechnologyGuidelines.html#//apple_ref/doc/uid/TP30000355-SW9.

How Can Natural Mapping Improve Usability?

Efficiency

Bad natural mapping can affect all three phases of the action cycle. The user must spend more time in the look phase to read the specific text on button labels, instead of quickly glancing at their overall position. The user must also spend more time in the think phase, considering what the label of each button means. Finally, it is also possible that the act phase could be delayed as the user tries different controls until they get the right one, due to the position of the controls feeling unnatural.

Learnability

Natural mapping can also improve learnability. If controls are laid out in a way that matches the action that they perform, as well as the user's mental model, the user will understand how the controls work much faster.[*]

Understanding Natural Mapping

A common keyboard configuration for first-person shooter games is WASD: pressing the "w" key moves you forward, "s" moves you back, and the "a" and "d" keys strafe left and right (see the left side of Figure 5.15). Because the movement is relative to the position of the keys, this is an example of good natural mapping.

Instead, imagine if the "w" and "s" keys strafe left and right, and the "a" and "d" keys move forward and backward (see the right side of Figure 5.15). When your opponent fires a rocket at you, and you press the "a" key expecting to go left, instead you walk right into it and explode into a ludicrous amount of giblets. You can imagine how frustrating that would be!

FIGURE 5.15 The standard WASD key configuration for first-person shooters.

---

[*] Furthermore, when it comes to memorability—the ability to remember how to use the tool after not having used it for a while—users tend to remember the general location of a control first (left side, right side, or middle of the toolbar), and then the label/icon associated with that control.

Moving forward with the "a" key does not feel natural, because it is to the left of the other keys. This would be an example of bad natural mapping.

What Are Examples of Patterns That Use Natural Mapping?

The Color Set Editor window in Autodesk Maya shows an example of good natural mapping. The "Move Up" and "Move Down" buttons are positioned relative to the actions that they perform (see the left side of Figure 5.16).

Another good example is the Connection Editor window. All of the buttons that are related to the left are positioned on the left, and all of the buttons that are related to the right are positioned on the right (see the middle of Figure 5.16).

However, there are times when limited space can lead to compromises to natural mapping, as can be seen in the Layers Editor. The buttons for moving layers up and down are placed side by side (see the right side of Figure 5.16). This is not ideal natural mapping.

REPRESENTATION

Representation is a technique that can be used to help users make quicker decisions without increasing time spent in the think phase of the action cycle (such as doing calculations in their heads). It is often most useful when the user interface does not match the user's mental model.

How Can Representation Improve Usability?
Efficiency
If the user has to do calculations in their head, they will spend a lot of time in the think phase. By presenting complex concepts in a simple way, they can spend more time in the act phase, increasing their efficiency.

Learnability
If the concepts in a tool are confusing for the user, they will have difficulty learning how to use it. By using representation to match the user's mental model, the interface more closely resembles how the users think, making it easier to learn.

Understanding Representation
The Numbers Game
To understand how we can use representation, we will play a game. You can also play this with a friend to explain the concept of representation.

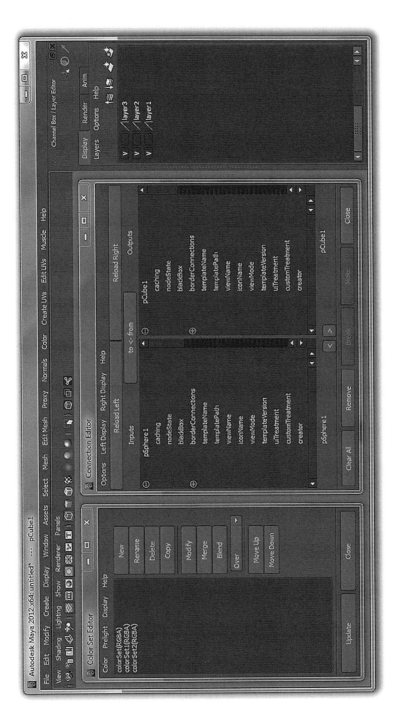

FIGURE 5.16 Examples of natural mapping across various editors of the Autodesk Maya interface. Autodesk screen shots reprinted with the permission of Autodesk, Inc.

$$1 \ \cancel{2} \ \cancel{3} \ \cancel{4} \ \cancel{5} \ \cancel{6} \ 7 \ \cancel{8} \ \cancel{9}$$
$$ \ \ \text{A} \ \ \text{B} \ \ \text{A} \ \ \text{A} \ \ \text{B} \ \ \ \ \ \text{A} \ \ \text{B}$$
$$8 + 2 + 5 = 15$$

FIGURE 5.17   An example of the numbers game.

First, one player writes down the numbers 1 through 9 on a piece of paper. Each player takes a turn choosing a number. They announce it to the other player and then cross it off the list. Once a number is chosen, it is no longer available.

The goal of the game is to keep picking numbers until one player can add up three of their numbers to make a total of 15. For example, the game could go like this (see Figure 5.17):

1. Player A picks 8

2. Player B picks 6

3. Player A picks 4

4. Player B picks 3

5. Player A picks 2

6. Player B picks 9

7. Player A picks 5

8. The game is over: Player B picked 8, 4, 2, and 5. They can make 15 by adding up the numbers 8, 2, and 5.

Does that sounds a little bit complicated? Now, imagine playing the game without writing anything down, and calculating the numbers in your head! Add to that the fact that you also have to remember if your opponent already picked a specific number.

Tic-Tac-Toe

Let's forget about the numbers game and play a completely different game: tic-tac-toe. By comparison, this game is very simple: you and your opponent take turns placing X's and O's on a three-by-three grid, and the first player to get three X's or O's in a horizontal, vertical, or diagonal line wins (see Figure 5.18). This is a game that anyone can learn in seconds and does not require doing any calculations in your head.

FIGURE 5.18   An example of tic-tac-toe.

Magic Square

Here is where it gets interesting: what if I told you that the two games we just saw—the numbers game and tic-tac-toe—are actually the same game?

A magic square is a three-by-three grid, with each space containing a different number from one to nine. If you add up the numbers diagonally, vertically, and horizontally, you always end up with 15 (see Figure 5.19).

Now, think back to the numbers game, and how complicated it is: remembering your own numbers, doing math in your head, and even having to remember what numbers your opponent picked. Now, if you simply play tic-tac-toe with a magic square, you can pick three numbers that add up to exactly 15 in a matter of seconds, with little effort.

That is the power of representation: presenting the user interface in such a way that it simplifies a complex concept, allowing the user to make decisions more quickly and easily.

What Are Examples of Patterns That Use Representation?

In previous versions of Microsoft Office, you had to use an interface similar to the one you see on the left in Figure 5.20 if you wanted to insert a new table.

This interface requires you to visualize the table in your head, think about how many rows and columns you want it to have, and then translate that into the numbers that you enter into the "Number of columns" and "Number of rows" fields.

8	1	6
3	5	7
4	9	2

15   15   15

FIGURE 5.19   An example of a magic square.

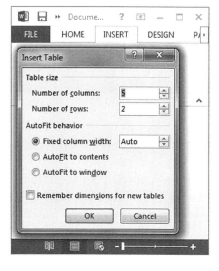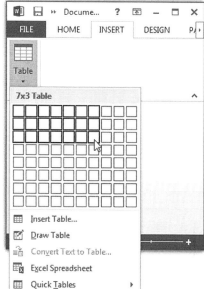

FIGURE 5.20   An example of using representation to insert a table in Microsoft Office. Used with permission from Microsoft.

Newer versions of Microsoft Office provide an interesting example of representation to build your table. This design allows the user to move their mouse inside a grid to set the number of rows and columns for their table visually, which matches most users' mental model of what a table is much more closely (see the right side of Figure 5.20).

Using this technique does have a small downside: it limits the total number of rows and columns the user can choose. This limit is likely based on the maximum number of columns and rows that the average user needs. For the edge case of an expert user who needs to go beyond the maximum, the "Insert Table…" menu item is still available just below the grid (see the right side of Figure 5.20, near the bottom).*

FEEDBACK

Feedback is all about how the tool communicates with the user. Examples of feedback include what the tool is doing now, what just happened, and how much time is left in a particular process.

---

* If the user needs hundreds of cells in a table, maybe Microsoft Word is not the right tool, and they should be using a tool that does one thing (spreadsheets) really well: Microsoft Excel.

How Can Feedback Improve Usability?

Efficiency

Feedback helps indirectly with efficiency because it lets the user know if they can do something else while they are waiting. Furthermore, the user is less likely to force close an application, requiring them to redo any work that they may have lost.

Learnability

In-context feedback through carefully worded messages can help the user learn how the tool works more quickly and make them more confident in their understanding of the tool.

Understanding Feedback

When two humans engage in conversation, there is an exchange of information. One person speaks, and the other listens. When one person is done speaking, the other person replies. We are accustomed to this from years of social interaction.

For example, a back-and-forth conversation might go something like this:

Mario: Hello, Luigi. It's-a me, Mario! How are you today?
Luigi: I am doing well. How are you?
Mario: I am doing very well, thank you for asking!

Now, imagine a conversation like this:

Mario: Hello, Luigi. It's-a me, Mario! How are you today?
Luigi: I am doing well. How are you?
Mario: … (stares at Luigi)
Luigi: Mario?
Mario: … (continues staring at Luigi)
Luigi: Mario, hello?
Mario: … (blinks once)
Luigi: … oookay … (walks away)

That would make for a very awkward conversation. As humans, we are not accustomed to interactions like this. We expect an almost instantaneous confirmation of our presence in our social interactions. We cannot fault Luigi for walking away.

Likewise, as you will recall from Chapter 4, an interaction between a human and computer is a back-and-forth process. The human performs an action, and the computer responds. The human sees what the computer did, and they perform the next action.

However, too often, the interaction between humans and computers resembles the awkward social interaction: the human performs an action, but the computer does not respond. Worse still, the user may think that the program has crashed and close it, losing all unsaved work.

Now, imagine a third conversation like this:

Mario: Hello, Luigi. How are you today?
Luigi: I am doing well. How are you?
Mario: Just a moment, let me think …
Luigi: Sure, I can wait.
Mario: …
Luigi: Are you still thinking?
Mario: Yep, just give me a minute.
Luigi: OK! No problem. Thanks for letting me know.
Mario: Sorry about that. I am doing very well, thank you for asking!

This interaction is less awkward. Luigi knows that Mario is still participating in the conversation but that he is not ready to respond quite yet. Luigi is unlikely to walk away.

Acceptable Response Time

Jakob Nielsen, whom we spoke about in Chapter 4, published a book in 1993 titled *Usability Engineering* where he describes three important limits when it comes to acceptable response times, with recommendations on when feedback is recommended:[*]

- At 0.1 second, the users "feel that the system is reacting instantaneously" and no feedback is necessary.

- 1 second "is about the limit for the user's flow of thought to stay uninterrupted." The user will notice the delay and will "lose the feeling of operating directly on the data," which can make the tool feel sluggish. In this case, a wait cursor is recommended.

---

[*] Here is an article with a summary of the information: http://www.nngroup.com/articles/response-times-3-important-limits/.

- 10 seconds is "the limit for keeping the user's attention." For anything longer, the user will forget what they were doing, which could affect their efficiency. In this case, users should receive feedback to confirm that the computer is working, and an estimate of how much longer they need to wait. Using a progress bar is ideal in this situation.

Perceived Wait Time

In 1985, while he was studying at the University of Toronto under Bill Buxton, Brad Allan Myers published a paper titled "The Importance of Percent-Done Progress Indicators for Computer–Human Interfaces."* The paper describes Myers's research on how progress bars affect our perception of time. In his experiment, he asked people to perform database searches, some of which had progress bars and some of which did not have them. The results of the study indicate that the participants felt more confident in the database searches with progress bars.

The Benefits of Giving the User Feedback

As we can see in the previous examples, giving the user feedback with a progress bar can help in multiple ways. It confirms to the user that the tool is still working—which stops them from forcing it to close and potentially losing unsaved work—and gives them the confidence to do something else while they are waiting, which increases their overall efficiency.

Furthermore, in Chapter 1 we learned how one of the qualities of a good user experience is when the interaction is "more human." If we compare our awkward conversation example from before to a long wait without a progress bar, we can see how waiting without feedback can result in a "less human" user experience.

Feedback Overload

One of the dangers of feedback is that it can quickly turn into more noise than signal. If you give the user too much feedback, they are likely to start ignoring all of it and miss something important. If you are aware of the user's goals and mental models, you can use that knowledge to filter the feedback you provide. If you are not, the feedback is likely to be overloaded with information that may be important for the conceptual model, but not to the user.

---

* Note the term "percent-done progress indicators"—at the time, progress bars did not exist as we know them now. You can find the paper here: http://dl.acm.org/citation.cfm?id=317459.

FIGURE 5.21 The progress bar in Windows gives feedback on the progress of a large file being pasted. Used with permission from Microsoft.

What Are Some Examples of Patterns That Use Feedback?

Progress Bar

Progress bars indicate the progress of a task and give us a sense of how much of the task is left.[*] Perhaps one of the most recognized is the copy progress bar in Microsoft Windows (see Figure 5.21).[†]

Some progress bars lock the tool while they are running. However, some can show a progress bar while still allowing the user to continue working. A good example of this is Adobe Audition: when running a multitrack mixdown, the editor is locked and a pie-chart progress indicator appears, with the estimated remaining time (see Figure 5.22). However, the user can still work on other aspects of the user interface while they are waiting.

Wait Cursor

Showing a wait cursor next to the mouse has the advantage of being easier for the user to notice, as their eyes are likely already on the mouse. However, since most wait cursors do not show progress, it is best to use this option when the wait time is relatively short.

FEED-FORWARD

Feed-forward is essentially the opposite of feedback: instead of learning the results of their actions after the fact, the user sees what will happen before they commit to an action. This gives them the option of changing their mind, which is especially useful if the action is destructive or complicated to reverse.

---

[*] Some research even suggests that animated patterns overlaid on top of the progress bar can make it feel as though it is moving faster! http://chrisharrison.net/projects/progressbars2/ProgressBarsHarrison.pdf.

[†] Microsoft's guidelines for progress bars can be seen here: http://msdn.microsoft.com/en-us/library/windows/desktop/dn742475%28v=vs.85%29.aspx.

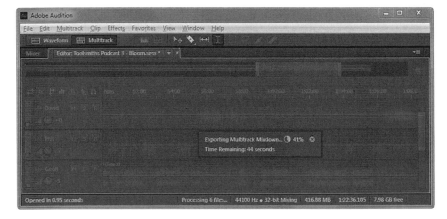

FIGURE 5.22 An integrated progress pie-chart gives feedback on the export progress in Adobe Audition. Adobe product screenshot(s) reprinted with permission from Adobe Systems Incorporated.

How Can Feed-Forward Improve Usability?

Efficiency

Feed-forward is especially helpful in reducing the amount of time spent in the think phase. There is no need to wonder what is going to happen, as you simply see it before you choose to commit.

Learnability

Feed-forward is an extremely effective learning technique. Previewing what will happen allows the user to learn what a feature does instantly and with less risk, which also invites them to explore the other features of the tool.

Understanding Feed-Forward

While the concept of feedback in user interfaces is well known, feed-forward is less so.[*] Research suggests that when people make a decision, their brain "previews" the outcome of their choices to assist in choosing the correct action.[†] In a sense, feed-forward helps us preview decisions in the same way that our brain does.

---

[*] One of the first uses of the term *feed-forward* in the context of user experience design comes from Tom Djajadiningrat, in his paper "But How, Donald, Tell Us How." If you have access to the ACM Digital Library, you can read the article here: http://dl.acm.org/citation.cfm?id=778752.

[†] You can read more here: http://en.wikipedia.org/wiki/Feedforward,_Behavioral_and_Cognitive_Science.

What Are Examples of Patterns That Use Feed-Forward?

A good example of a pattern that uses feed-forward is the Styles section of the ribbon in Microsoft Word. By hovering their mouse over each style, the user can get a preview of what their text will look like with the style applied directly in their document (see the top of Figure 5.23). However, they do not have to commit to the decision. If they are not satisfied, they simply move the mouse to another style (see the middle of Figure 5.23) or out of the Styles section completely (see the bottom of Figure 5.23). However, once they find the style they like, they can click to commit to it. This is much more efficient than applying a style, undoing, applying a style, undoing, and so on.

When attempting to drag and drop a material onto objects in the Unity game engine viewport, the objects under the mouse are shown with the material instantly, as opposed to only after you release the mouse button (see Figure 5.24).

The numbers that indicate how many items are inside a folder is another example of feed-forward. For example, the folder list in Gmail shows how many unread mail items there are in each category (see Figure 5.25), allowing the user to skip over folders that do not contain unread items instead of taking the time to check each one.

GROUPING

Grouping is the technique of associating similar terms, concepts, or commands together in a way that matches the user's mental model.

How Can Grouping Improve Usability?

Efficiency

By grouping related items together, the user can scan through a list of items and find what they are looking for more quickly, reducing the amount of time spent in the look phase. This could also reduce the think phase, because fewer items to look at mean fewer items to think about.

Learnability

Grouping can make a tool easier to learn because the interface is organized in a logical way that matches how the user thinks, allowing them to adapt to it faster.

FIGURE 5.23   Using feed-forward to preview changes to formatting in Microsoft Word. Used with permission from Microsoft.

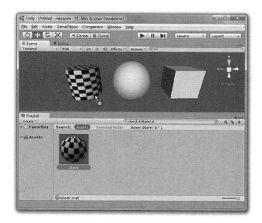

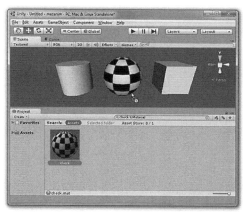

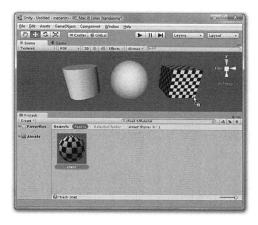

FIGURE 5.24   Feed-forward allows the user to preview how a material will change the look of an object in the Unity Engine before committing to the change.

FIGURE 5.25 Feed-forward gives the user information about the contents of a folder in Gmail without requiring them to click on it. Google and the Google logo are registered trademarks of Google Inc., used with permission.

Understanding Grouping

Grouping is one of the many techniques that make up the discipline of information architecture. The most important factor in determining how terms, concepts, and commands can be grouped is by understanding the user's mental model.

For example, by using separators, menu items can be organized to reflect how the user associates them. This allows the user to skip the menu items that are not applicable to their immediate goals and find what they are looking for faster.

Some people may look at the concept of grouping menu items and say, "Well, that's just associating similar commands together!" That may be true, but how they are associated is not always obvious. We may have an opinion on how the menus should be organized, but we could be influenced by the way the data is organized in the code, and not how the user thinks about it. To help us determine how to group information from the user's perspective, we can do a card sort.

Using a Card Sort to Determine Groups

In Chapter 4, we learned about how card sorting can help us understand the user's mental model. The way in which a user associates menu items is also part of their mental model. By putting each command in our menu onto a set of cards, and asking the user to organize them, we can get a much better idea as to how they associate each of the commands.

When you are done, study the results and look for common trends. For example, did the majority of users put all of the commands that create polygon and NURBS primitives together, or did they combine the create polygon primitives and polygon editing tools together into one group?

Afterward, you can transform the groups into top-level menus and the cards into individual menu items.

This process can be applied to window menus, contextual menus, toolbars, and so on.

What Are Examples of Patterns That Use Grouping?

The menu items in Autodesk Maya are grouped in such a way that matches the user's mental model (see Figure 5.26). For example, even though the

FIGURE 5.26   The Mesh menu in Autodesk Maya demonstrates the technique of grouping. Autodesk screen shots reprinted with the permission of Autodesk, Inc.

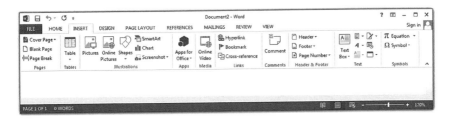

FIGURE 5.27 Grouping is used to organize commands in the Microsoft Office ribbon. Used with permission from Microsoft.

"Smooth" command adds new vertices to the selected mesh, and the "Average Vertices" command moves vertices, they are grouped together because they are both related to giving the mesh a smoother appearance.

In addition, all of the commands related to transferring information from one mesh to another are grouped together. If the user is scanning the list of commands and is not planning to transfer information, they can skip over that whole section to the next group.

The Microsoft ribbon shows yet another example of grouping. At the top level, the commands in the ribbon are organized into tabs. For example, all commands related to inserting charts or external resources to a Microsoft Word document can be found under the "INSERT" tab. If the user wants to insert a chart to their document, they can quickly skip over the "VIEW" or "REFERENCES" tabs, as they do not contain the commands they are looking for (see the top of the ribbon in Figure 5.27).

One level below are the sections. If we return to the example of the "INSERT" tab, we have a series of sections for different elements that can be inserted: Pages, Tables, Illustrations, and so on (see the bottom of the ribbon in Figure 5.27). These are grouped together in a way that the average user may expect. This way, if the user is looking to insert an illustration, they can skip over all of the commands within the "Pages" and "Tables" groups and go directly to the commands within the "Illustrations" group.

CHUNKING

You may have heard the statistic that people are able to remember seven items at once, plus or minus two. This number comes from research by George A. Miller in 1956 and is often referred to as "Miller's Law."[*]

---

[*] You can read more about Miller's Law here: http://en.wikipedia.org/wiki/Miller%27s_law.

However, new research suggests that this number is closer to four, plus or minus two. The reason that Miller's numbers were higher is that his research subjects were able to clump similar items together, making them easier to remember. This behavior is known as "chunking."

How Can Chunking Improve Usability?

Efficiency

If the information is organized in a consistent way, the user can remember and interpret it more easily, resulting in less time spent in the think phase.

Learnability

If the information is organized in such a way that matches the user's mental model, learnability can be improved.

Understanding Chunking

To feel the difference that chunking can make, we will play a memory game. Study the image of letters and numbers in Figure 5.28 for ten seconds, and try to remember as many as you can.

After the ten seconds are up, close the book and get a piece of paper and a pen. First, write down how many letters and numbers you think that there were. Next, try to write down as many of the letters and numbers you can remember. When you are a ready, turn to the next page.

In Figure 5.28, you can see the exact same letters and numbers as in Figure 5.29. Imagine that you were asked to study those same letters and numbers for ten seconds, but in this configuration. How many do you think you would be able to recall? Would you get them all right?

The fact that it is easier for you to remember those same letters and numbers this way is an example of chunking: You have a predefined structure in your brain for the shortened names of these video game consoles. It is easier to remember and decipher the letters and numbers when you can group them together in a logical way that makes sense to you.

4EISNW6NSI

FIGURE 5.28 Memory game.

SNES N64 WII

FIGURE 5.29   Memory game, with chunking.

What Are Examples of Patterns That Use Chunking?

Content creation tools allow users to work with RGBA color values in different ways: 0 to 255, 0.0 to 1.0, and hexadecimal. Despite the fact that hexadecimal does not match the mental model of color for the average person, it has become a standard for working with certain types of content.

When users are accustomed to working with hexadecimal, they are able to pick out the red, green, blue, and alpha values quickly by chunking the characters in groups of two. For example, a user familiar with RGBA in hexadecimal can look at the value #FF7F00FF and determine very quickly that the color has 100 percent red (the first and second characters) and 50 percent blue (the third and fourth characters).

However, some tools do not work with hexadecimal colors in RGBA—such as Microsoft Expression Blend, which uses ARGB.* This can be confusing to users who are accustomed to chunking RGBA colors. The previous color would appear to be 100 percent red, 100 percent blue, 50 percent green, and fully transparent to someone who is used to working with RGBA!

When designing how information will appear to the user, consider how they will chunk it. Also, try to follow existing standards. If technical limitations make this impossible, make the information familiar and easier to chunk for the user in the interface, and then convert it to the necessary format in the background so the user does not have to think about it.

EXCISE

Excise refers to navigating around the interface, from switching tabs to changing windows. Anything that involves moving the cursor across the screen to reach an element of the user interface is excise.

How Can This Technique Improve Usability?

Efficiency

Reducing excise will have the biggest impact on the act phase of the action cycle. Although it is the lightest load, reducing a repetitive task even by

---

* This is likely because it was designed to work with the XAML file format, which uses ARGB.

one second can add up to a huge boost in efficiency over time if it helps a large number of users.

Learnability
Excise does not have a significant impact on learnability.

Understanding Excise

One of the most consistently confirmed studies in human–computer interaction was completed in 1954 by Paul Fitts, who proposed that the time it takes a user to touch a target with a cursor is directly related to the distance from the target and the size of the target. This is known as Fitts's Law.[*]

Therefore, to reduce excise, the target must be made larger and/or closer to the current position of the cursor.

What Are Examples of Patterns That Use Excise?

Window Menus Versus Contextual Menus

Accessing items in a menu or toolbar frequently is an example of excise that is mainly related to target distance. The user must move their cursor to the menu or toolbar and click on the item and then move the cursor back to where it was before (see top of Figure 5.30).[†]

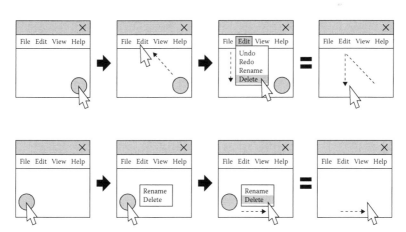

FIGURE 5.30   Comparing the excise of a window menu (top) versus a contextual menu (bottom).

---

[*] You can read more about Fitts's Law here: http://en.wikipedia.org/wiki/Fitts%27s_law.
[†] Specifications for menus and contextual menus from Microsoft can be found here: http://msdn. microsoft.com/en-us/library/windows/desktop/dn742392%28v=vs.85%29.aspx.

By comparison, contextual menus can help to reduce excise because they appear right next to the user's cursor, resulting in shorter distance (see the bottom of Figure 5.30). In addition, as the name "contextual menu" implies, only items that are contextually related to the item that was clicked should be enabled in the menu, which means a shorter list, and therefore a shorter distance to the option that the user is looking for.

Window Menu Item Order

While it might seem that organizing menu items alphabetically will make it easy to find a specific menu item, this approach presents two problems. The first is that the menu rarely matches how the user chunks information. The second is that the items that are accessed more frequently may be further from the cursor, because the first letter of the command is near the end of the alphabet.

For example, the level editor GTKRadiant has a contextual menu with items that are ordered alphabetically. If the majority of users are frequently required to create entities of type "worldspawn," they must move their mouse to the bottom of the contextual menu every single time, which results in a lot of excise (see the left of Figure 5.31).

Another very common situation is having menu items listed in the order that they were created. In other words, when a developer adds a new command, it is placed at the bottom of the menu (see the right of Figure 5.31).

A better solution is to place the most frequently used commands at the top of the menu, reducing the travel time from the point at which the menu was raised (see Figure 5.32). When new items are added, learn the frequency at which they will be used—either by looking at metrics or by doing a task analysis—and place them in the appropriate position in the menu. This can apply to window menus, contextual menus, combo boxes, menu buttons, and more.

Bottom of the Screen

There is one problem with ordering items in a contextual menu from top to bottom: the mouse is not always at the top! Sometimes, a user will invoke a contextual menu from the bottom of the screen, and the contex-

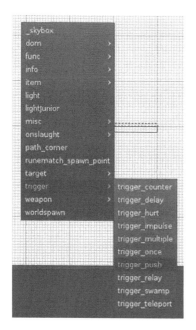

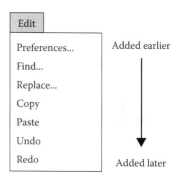

FIGURE 5.31 Two ways in which the organization of a contextual menu can increase excise: Alphabetical, as in GTKRadiant (left) or the order in which the commands were added (right).

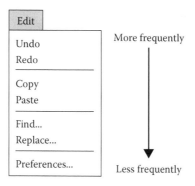

FIGURE 5.32 Organizing a menu based upon how often the commands are used can reduce excise.

tual menu will appear above the mouse, instead of below it. What can be done about this?

Microsoft Office presents an interesting solution to this problem: frequently used formatting commands appear in a floating bar that changes position depending on where the contextual menu was invoked. When

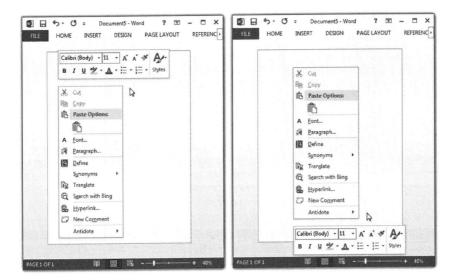

FIGURE 5.33 The contextual menu in Microsoft Office changes based upon where it was invoked in an effort to minimize excise. Used with permission from Microsoft.

the cursor is at the top of the window, the floating bar appears at the top, nearer to the cursor (see the left side of Figure 5.33). However, when the cursor is at the bottom, the floating bar appears at the bottom (see the right side of Figure 5.33).

The marking menu in Autodesk Maya is yet another approach to reducing excise (see Figure 5.34). Marking menus typically have up to eight regions,* which are all the same distance from the cursor.

Contextual Menus and Learning Curve
When considering the use of contextual menus, do not forget about the learning curve concepts that were presented in Chapter 4. Because contextual menus are not always visible, they are difficult to discover for beginners. For this reason, it is best to ensure that the most frequently used commands are always visible in toolbars or menus so new users can find them.

---

* While the number of options on the menu is limited to eight, commands can be chained together. However, that technique is geared more toward expert users.

FIGURE 5.34 The marking menu in Autodesk Maya is excellent at reducing excise, though it can be difficult for beginner users. Autodesk screen shots reprinted with the permission of Autodesk, Inc.

Examples of Target Size

For an example of target size, we can look at Adobe Premiere Pro (see Figure 5.35). One of the most frequent actions is pressing the play button, while one of the least common actions is closing the sequence that you are currently working on.

Because the play button is a large target, it is easy to acquire with the mouse. By comparison, the close button for a sequence is only a few pixels across, making it difficult to click by accident.

FIGURE 5.35 The size difference of the "play" and "close sequence" buttons in Adobe Premiere demonstrates the concept of target size excise. Adobe product screenshot(s) reprinted with permission from Adobe Systems Incorporated.

Hotkeys and Excise

While it may be true that using hotkeys to activate a command can reduce excise as compared to moving the mouse to click on a button, reaching keys on the keyboard can be excise too!

A complicated hotkey combination such as Ctrl/Cmd+Alt+P cannot be done one-handed by most users. It may require the user to look down at the keyboard and take their other hand off the mouse. This may not seem like much, but if the hotkey is for a command that is used often, it can add up to lost efficiency like any other kind of excise.

Resting Place

Any pro gamer can tell you that optimal hotkey placement is crucial to efficiency. All of the default hotkeys for the competitive multiplayer RTS *Starcraft* are placed along the left side of the keyboard, near the resting

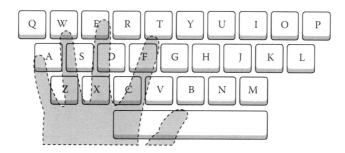

FIGURE 5.36 Considering the resting place of the left hand when choosing hotkeys.

place of the left hand.* In the case where efficiency is not important, choosing a hotkey based on the first letter of the command would make sense, such as using "M" to build a marine. However, to make the player more efficient, the second letter in the word *marine* is used: "A," because it is on the left side of the keyboard, near the resting place of the left hand (see Figure 5.36).

You can see the same rules applied to content creation tools. For example, the majority of 3D content creation applications use the letters Q, W, E, and R for select, move, rotate, and scale, respectively, which are some of the commands that are used most frequently. Another classic example is undo, copy, cut, and paste: Ctrl/Cmd+Z, X, C, and V.†

When choosing hotkeys for the commands that are used most frequently, try to choose hotkeys that are near the left side of the keyboard. If the key for the first letter of the command is on the right side, or is already used, then use the next letter in the name of the command. Also, to avoid confusion, don't replace standard hotkeys like the ones for undo, copy, cut, and paste that are listed above, as well as Ctrl/Cmd+S, O, W, and A for save, open, close, and select all, respectively.

Deliberately Increasing Excise to Protect the User

There may be times when you want to increase excise on purpose. This may be to slow down the user so that they have more time to think about a

---

* As left-handed people already know, most default hotkeys are made with right-handed people in mind. If there are a significant number of left-handed users, you can give the option to customize the keyboard so the resting place is on the right side instead.

† Of course, all of this is assuming a North American QWERTY layout. Other layouts like AZERTY would alter these rules a little bit.

potentially dangerous decision or to protect them from accidental actions. Here are a few options.

Dialog Boxes

There is a commonly held belief that dialog boxes should never be used, and that the fewer dialog boxes you have, the better. However, dialog boxes can be useful for protecting the user from errors. One such example is a dialog box confirming that you want to delete a file. Accidental clicks resulting in data loss can be reduced by forcing the user to change their focus to the dialog box, move their mouse, and click.

It is extremely important to note that a dialog box should be avoided in the case of commands that are used frequently. The slowdown in efficiency may be worse than the lack of error protection. In these cases, allowing the user to recover or undo their choice is highly recommended.

Potentially Dangerous Menu Items

Menu items that have the potential to cause irreversible damage—such as deleting an object—can be placed at the bottom of a menu, adding excise to protect the user from clicking on them by accident.

Inconvenient Hotkeys

Deliberately increasing the excise for a hotkey can also protect the user. For example, using the spacebar as a hotkey for a dangerous command that cannot be reversed would be a very bad idea. By comparison, a complex hotkey such as Ctrl/Cmd+Alt+P usually requires two hands and therefore has a significantly lower chance of being pressed accidentally.

However, there are a few exceptions: standards such as the "delete" key to delete should not be changed to protect the user, as they are so common that changing them would just lead to confusion. Again, the best way to protect against this is to implement a robust undo system.

PROGRESSIVE DISCLOSURE

Progressive disclosure means showing only the parts of the interface that the user needs to see. The interface starts simple, and we allow the user to reveal (disclose) more, one piece at a time (progressively), to suit their needs.

How Can Progressive Disclosure Improve Usability?

Efficiency

Progressive disclosure can reduce the amount of time spent in the look phase by reducing visual clutter in the interface. Furthermore, the less we see, the less we have to figure out, resulting in less time spent in the think phase. However, since showing and hiding can increase the amount of excise—in other words, time spent in the act phase—it is important to find the right balance between the amount of progressive disclosure and excise.

Learnability

Progressive disclosure is one of the most powerful techniques for improving learnability. By simplifying the interface, first-time users can get a grasp of how a tool works without being overwhelmed by all of the features at once, and expert users can customize the interface to suit their needs.

Understanding Progressive Disclosure

In Chapter 3, we spoke about how new features add complexity exponentially, not linearly. The same goes for the number of interface elements that are visible at one time. By starting with a simple and clean interface, and allowing the user to see more as they gain more experience, we are allowing the user to control the amount of complexity.

Progressive Disclosure and the Learning Curve

To decide if progressive disclosure is the right technique to use, you must first look at how many interface elements there are and how often they will be used.

For example, for a tool that has many interface elements and will be used all day by beginners as well as experts, using progressive disclosure makes sense. Beginners appreciate an interface that starts simple and accessible, and experts benefit from an interface that is powerful and customizable.

However, if the tool has a smaller number of interface elements, and is going to be used for five minutes, once per week—for example, a tool to update to the latest version of the game engine—progressive disclosure may not provide significant benefits.

FIGURE 5.37   Progressive disclosure can be used to hide information that most users may not be interested in, such as technical details about the "paste" process. Used with permission from Microsoft.

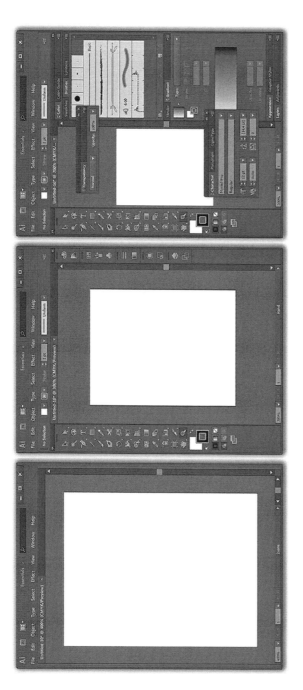

FIGURE 5.38 The variety of ways in which the interface of most Adobe products can be customized is an excellent example of progressive disclosure, and is appropriate for their level of complexity. Adobe product screenshot(s) reprinted with permission from Adobe Systems Incorporated.

What Are Some Examples of Patterns That Use Progressive Disclosure?

Progressive disclosure is such an established pattern that Microsoft has an entire section in their user experience guidelines dedicated to it.* As a result, you can find examples of this technique being used to show and hide elements all over Windows. For example, when pasting a large file, most users only want to know if the operation is done (see the top of Figure 5.37). However, for users who want to know more—such as precisely how much time is remaining, and the file transfer speed—they can click on the "More details" expander (see the bottom of Figure 5.37). In addition, when the paste dialog appears, the expander is closed by default, since this information does not interest most users.

It should not come as a surprise to see extensive use of progressive disclosure in Adobe products such as Photoshop and Illustrator, as they are extremely complex and have many different interface elements. To address this, each panel can be individually expanded and collapsed to show exactly what the user needs to accomplish their task (see Figure 5.38).

WRAPPING UP

In this chapter, we concentrated on the Design phase of the User-Centered Design process. We learned about how the brain and the eyes work together and how humans have evolved to see specific patterns more efficiently. We learned about the importance of using a consistent, clear visual language, and we also discovered the value of following design guidelines. Finally, we learned a wide variety of design techniques, such as Hierarchy, Constraints, Natural Mapping, Representation, Feedback, Feed-forward, Grouping, Chunking, Excise, and Progressive Disclosure.

In the next chapter, we will discuss concepts and techniques to be used during the Evaluation phase of the User-Centered Design process.

---

* You can find it here: http://msdn.microsoft.com/en-us/library/windows/desktop/dn742409 %28v=vs.85%29.aspx.

CHAPTER 6

Evaluation

WHAT WILL WE LEARN IN THIS CHAPTER?

Concepts

- Choosing the right evaluation strategy

- Deciding between code and pre-visualization

Techniques

- Pre-visualize the interface

- How to do a heuristic evaluation

- Performing user tests

HOW DO WE EVALUATE THE DESIGN?

Now that we have analyzed how the users use the tool and designed one or more improvements, it is time for the Evaluation phase. One of the first questions to ask ourselves is if it will be more cost-effective to go straight to code or to pre-visualize the changes to the tool. The next question to ask is if there are current users or users with a similar profile available to validate the interface. If users are available, we can do user tests. If not, we can perform a heuristic evaluation while we wait for users to become available.

CHOOSING BETWEEN CODE OR PRE-VISUALIZATION

In Chapter 2, we learned about Jeff Hawkins and the power of pre-visualizing. You might be asking yourself, "If pre-visualizing is so powerful, why not use it all the time?"

If you are not a programmer and there are no programmers on your team, or if there are programmers but they do not have time during the current sprint, your only option is to pre-visualize. This will allow you to start getting feedback from the users while you wait for programming resources to become available.

However, if you can program or if programmers are available, your decision to code or pre-visualize will depend on your situation. Here are a few aspects to consider.

When to Pre-Visualize

Pre-visualization is recommended if the estimated time to make changes to the tool is higher than the time it would take to pre-visualize. For example, it takes a lot less time to sketch out a new type of user interface control that has never been created before compared to fully implementing it in code.

If your goal is to measure the improvement to learnability, pre-visualization can be a good choice. For example, the design techniques of representation and hierarchy can be simulated by using pre-visualization with good accuracy.

However, pre-visualization is not ideal for measuring improvements to efficiency compared to making changes directly to the code. This is because pre-visualization techniques cannot simulate the response time of a real computer, and, in the case of a sketch, using your finger to press a button is not the same as clicking on the button with the mouse.

Furthermore, it is difficult to simulate a large database with pre-visualization. For example, if your user test requires that the user is able to search through a database containing thousands of textures, it could take significantly longer to pre-visualize every possible option. In these cases, you may choose to go straight to code.

When to Code

As we learned earlier, if your main goal is to improve efficiency, the best way to measure this accurately is by making changes to the code, due to the limited ability of pre-visualization to simulate the complete experience of using a tool.

If the changes are relatively small, such as moving around a few controls in the interface, this may also be a reason to make the changes directly in code. This is because the time it would take to simulate such a small change to the interface through pre-visualization may be higher.

However, if the changes that you want to make require a large programming effort and your main interest is seeing if the users understand and appreciate the new interface, going straight to code could be more expensive in the long term, especially if the users do not like the design in the end. In this case, pre-visualization may be the best choice.

PRE-VISUALIZE THE INTERFACE

If you have decided to pre-visualize instead of going straight to code, here are a few techniques that you can use.

Sketch

Sketches are one of the quickest ways to pre-visualize (see Figure 6.1). They could be on a whiteboard, in a notebook, or even on a napkin. Because they are so fast to create, they are ideal for trying out a variety of different options. It does not matter how you sketch, as long as you are turning words into visuals in an effort to have a shared vision of the design.

You do not have to be a good artist to sketch. In fact, if the sketch looks like it did not take a lot of time to create and it is easy to change, people are more likely to be honest with their feedback, which is exactly what you want.

However, one of the reasons that sketches are fast to create is because they are not interactive, and they contain the least amount of detail compared to other pre-visualization options. This could lead to problems during the evaluation, if the lack of interactivity and details impairs the user's ability to understand the interface. The choice to use sketches depends on the complexity of the design that you are evaluating.

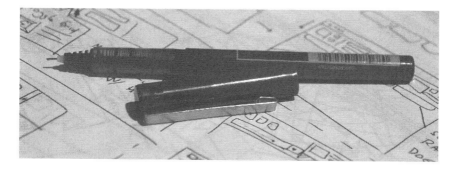

FIGURE 6.1   Sketches are a quick and easy way to pre-visualize the interface.

FIGURE 6.2   Paper prototype, using the "Wizard of Oz" technique.

Paper Prototype

Paper prototypes are essentially interactive sketches. We can use pen, paper, cardboard, scissors, tape, sticky notes, and other materials to create and simulate interactive elements (see Figure 6.2).

To make a paper prototype interactive, we can use what is called the "Wizard of Oz" technique. The name comes from the movie of the same name, because the interactivity is created by someone "behind the curtain." This technique works best with two people: one person asks the user to accomplish a specific task, and the other simulates the interactivity by moving pieces of the paper prototype around in reaction to the user's actions.*

Simulating interaction with a paper prototype has a few advantages over code: Paper prototypes never get compiler or linking errors. The only thing you need to deploy them are your own two legs. They are easily portable and can be archived indefinitely in a file folder. Finally, anyone can create a paper prototype without having to learn a programming language or a graphic design tool.†

---

* To see an example of this in action, watch this video: http://www.youtube.com/watch?v= GrV2SZuRPv0.
† In fact, there is an old joke among user experience designers: if you have ever done arts and crafts in kindergarten, you can create a paper prototype.

Interactive Prototype

These prototypes are created and evaluated on a computer or other device, using interactive prototype creation tools.* These tools come prepackaged with standard controls such as buttons, drop-downs, and checkboxes. Most allow you to add simple interactions, such as opening a dialog box when clicking a button (see Figure 6.3).

Although they cannot simulate every single type of interaction, most interactive prototype creation tools have very powerful and versatile systems for building interactions, as well as vibrant communities where people share recipes to simulate different types of behaviors.

In addition, if your users are not in the same building—or even the same country—interactive prototypes are clearly a better choice compared to sketches and paper prototypes, as they can be shared electronically. By using screen sharing, you can even watch people test the prototype in real time and get feedback as if you were sitting next to them.

Interactive prototypes can bring you closer to simulating the real tool as compared to sketches and paper prototypes. If you are simulating a tool that will be used on a desktop computer, interactive prototypes are about as close as you can get to reality without actually writing code.

However, there are a few drawbacks to interactive prototypes. For most people new to user experience design, building an interactive prototype requires learning a new tool. In addition, making changes can sometimes be more complicated compared to a sketch or paper prototype. There is also the chance that deploying a prototype on somebody else's computer will not work at first. For this reason, it is recommended to test out interactive prototypes on another machine before doing a large number of user tests.

PERFORM A HEURISTIC EVALUATION

In Chapter 1, we learned—through the user experience pyramid—that one of the foundations of a good user experience is usability. Heuristic evaluation can be a useful technique when there are no users available to evaluate the interface. It allows us to catch usability problems before the users do.

---

* Two of the most popular professional tools are Axure and Balsamiq, which you can find at http://www.axure.com and http://www.balsamiq.com, respectively. Another alternative is to import a series of static screenshots into Microsoft PowerPoint, Apple Keynote, or Adobe Acrobat and make them interactive by creating clickable hotspots.

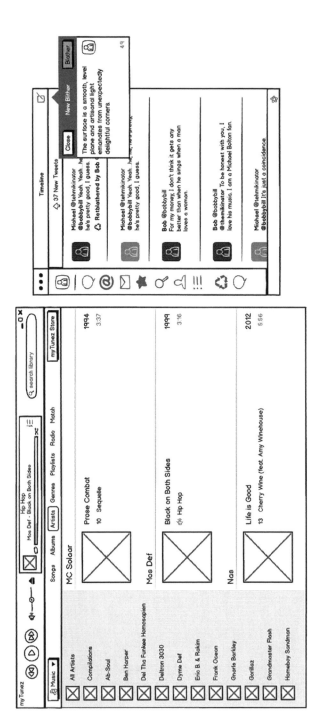

FIGURE 6.3   An example of an interactive prototype. Balsamiq is a registered trademark of Giacomo Guilizzoni, licensed to Balsamiq SRL and Balsamiq Studios, LLC, used with permission.

Although there are many varieties of usability heuristics,[*] for the purposes of this book, we will learn the heuristics established by Jakob Nielsen in 1994, which are perhaps the most popular and widely used. They originate from his book *Usability Engineering.*[†]

The heuristics are listed in the following sections. For each one, you will find a quote of what someone might say when confronting this heuristic, one or more examples to help you identify the heuristic, as well as design techniques from the previous chapter that could be used to improve the problem.

What Are the Heuristics?
Visibility of System Status
"What is the tool doing right now? Did it crash?" There are no progress bars or wait cursors. The tool freezes while it is performing an action without telling the user to wait. There are no dialogs to inform the user of what is going on. For this heuristic, the technique of feedback is recommended to keep the user informed of what the tool is doing.

Match between System and Real World
"I don't understand what this means." The words and concepts used in the tool are confusing, because they do not match the user's mental model. In addition, the position of the controls does not make sense relative to their functionality (for example, up and down buttons are placed side by side). In the case of this heuristic, natural mapping and representation can help make the tool easier to understand by matching the users' mental model more closely.

User Control and Freedom
"How do I go back to where I was before?" When a mistake is made, there is no clear way to go back to where you were before. Another common sign: the tool does not support undo/redo. In this case, the technique of feed-forward can help. This is because it allows the user to see what their action will do, which gives them the option to change their mind before it is too late.

---

[*] Here are a few: http://en.wikipedia.org/wiki/Heuristic_evaluation, as well as those by Bastien & Scapin: http://www.webmaestro.gouv.qc.ca/publications/archives/webeducation1998-2004/2000-11/criteres.pdf.

[†] You can read more about Nielsen's heuristics here: http://www.nngroup.com/articles/ten-usability-heuristics/.

Consistency and Standards

"Is this the same as that?" Two similar controls that edit the same type of data do not work the same way. For example, one list box may only delete selected items with the delete key on the keyboard, whereas the other list box within the same tool only deletes selected items with a delete button in the interface. As opposed to a specific design technique, the best way to address this heuristic is to ensure that the tool follows guidelines and uses interaction patterns consistently.

Error Prevention

"How can I prevent that mistake from happening again?" The interface makes it far too easy for mistakes to occur, such as allowing an item to be dragged and dropped where it is not supposed to, or setting the default button for a "Exit without save changes?" dialog box to "Yes." The design techniques of constraints and feed-forward can be useful for fixing issues associated with this heuristic. In addition, by strategically increasing excise, you can give the user more time to consider their options and prevent them from making mistakes.

Recognition Rather Than Recall

"I can't remember what it was called. If I had a list of options to choose from …" The tool does not provide a visual preview for a list of 3D meshes, so the only way to know what they are is to open them one at a time. Another common example is forcing the user to remember syntax or object names instead of providing suggestions. This not only hurts efficiency but also can lead to errors. The design technique of representation can be useful here, since it can be used to help the user remember what they were looking for by showing them a list of options.

Flexibility and Efficiency of Use

"I wish there was a faster way to do this." Actions that need to be performed very frequently do not have shortcuts, such as a hotkey or a prominent button in the interface. Improving excise is one of the most common ways to help address problems associated with this heuristic.

Aesthetic and Minimalist Design

"Whoa, this interface is complicated. I don't know where to start!" Every possible feature is exposed at once, and the user does not know where to look first. Furthermore, there is no way to hide or simplify the user interface for the first-time user. In the case of this heuristic, the design techniques of hierarchy and progressive disclosure could be used, as they can help guide the eye of the user, as well as letting them determine how much visual complexity they need in the interface.

Help Users Recognize, Diagnose, and Recover from Errors

"An error occurred. What do I do now?" Error messages do not clearly indicate what the problem is or help the user to find a solution. In this case, the recommended design techniques would be a combination of feedback (to let the user know how to fix the error) and constraints (to help the user avoid making the mistake in the first place).

Help and Documentation

"I'm stuck, and there's no one around that I can ask. What do I do?" No documentation, such as a wiki page, training video, or help file, is available. There is no clearly marked place to ask for assistance or log a bug. The design technique of feedback can be used in the form of contextual help within the application, often seen as little question marks near a user interface element to learn more about how it works.

How to Perform a Heuristic Evaluation

In an ideal situation, a heuristic evaluation is done by a large number of qualified user experience designers, who then combine their efforts to find as many usability problems as possible. However, doing a heuristic evaluation by yourself, or with a few members of the tools development team, may be better than not doing it at all.

To perform a heuristic evaluation, look at the pre-visualization or the working tool that you want to evaluate, and search for issues similar to those from the list of heuristics. It can be helpful to do this by stepping through the task flows that you created during the Analysis phase.

When you notice an issue that matches one of the heuristics, indicate the name of the heuristic and write a short description. Optionally, you can take a screenshot of the specific part of the interface that exhibits the problem. You can also assign a level of severity, to indicate how much this could affect the usability of the tool. This can help to prioritize what to improve first.

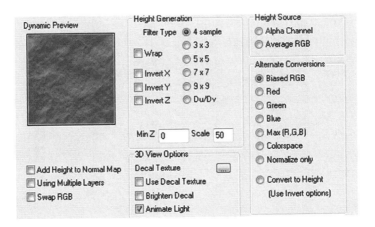

FIGURE 6.4 Heuristic evaluation of the NVIDIA Normal Map filter.

For example, if we were to do a heuristic evaluation on the NVIDIA Normal Map tool (see Figure 6.4), we might identify the following issues:

- Aesthetic and minimalist design: All of the options are displayed at once. Beginners do not know where to look first, which can be very intimidating. Severity: High.

- Consistency and standards: The "Alternate Conversions" section has more than seven radio buttons. Microsoft's design guidelines suggest using a drop-down when there are more than seven options. Severity: Low.

- Error prevention: The "Use Decal Texture" option can be checked even when there is no texture selected. This could lead to the user wondering why they cannot see their decal texture. Severity: Medium.

These are just a few examples, and you may be able to identify other issues with this particular interface.

Finally, remember that people use tools in unexpected ways. Doing a heuristic evaluation is a good first pass when no users are available. However, you should make every effort to follow it up by testing with users. Someone will work with the tool eventually, and the sooner you can watch them work, the better!

DO USER TESTS

One of the best ways to evaluate the user experience is by doing a user test. The first step to doing this is to build a test plan and select the users to test. Then, you need to prepare the interface that the users will evaluate, either by making changes directly in the code or by pre-visualizing. Finally, you can run the tests and examine the results in the next Analysis phase.

Building a Test Plan

The simplest kind of test plan is simply a list of tasks that you assign to the user. If you are building a test plan for the first time, you can get an idea of which tasks to include by looking at the user and stakeholder goals, as well as the task flows and scenario storyboards that you created during the Analysis phase. All of these can be used to help you determine which tasks you will ask the users to perform.

How to Phrase Tasks

A task should be phrased in the form of a question such as "How would you do this?" as opposed to a command: "Now do that." This is a closer match for the way people think when they are trying to achieve their goals.

For example, imagine that one of the user goals identified during a contextual inquiry is to create a new mesh with a shader assigned and add it to the level. Three tasks are required to accomplish this goal: create the mesh, add a shader, and add it to the level. In this case, you could phrase the three tasks as follows: "How would you create a mesh?", "How would you add a shader to the object?", and "How would you add the object to the level?"

Don't Assign Leading Tasks

In the Analysis phase, we discussed the danger of asking leading questions, and the same applies to user tests. If the question influences the user, you could get inaccurate results. For example, a leading task would be, "Use the object list to search for a tree, then drag and drop it into the level." The question implies where to find the tree and how to add it. A better alternative would be "You need to add a tree to the level. How would you do that?"

Realism and Context

It is also important to make the questions realistic and to give them context. For example, "How would you add a skyscraper in the middle of the forest in this level?" could result in unusual feedback since it is not a very realistic task.

Asking the user, "How would you add a large tree to the forest in this level?" is good, but an even better alternative would be, "The art director has requested that a large tree be added to the forest. How would you do that?" This question is more realistic, and the fact that the request comes from the art director adds context that is appropriate to that task.

Specific Tasks Are Easier to Measure

It is important that the tasks are as specific as possible. This allows the results of the user test to be compared not only between users but also across future iterations of the Evaluation phase. For example, the results of the task "How would you create a new shader?" could vary wildly if the user adds a default shader versus a complex ocean shader requiring several texture maps and customized properties for water movement. The task "How would you create a lambert shader with a prebuilt texture in the diffuse channel?" is much more specific and therefore can be measured and compared with more accuracy.

Select the Users

To select which users to test, you can use the same approach as the Analysis phase. Pick users who have a profile appropriate to the tasks. To get the most accurate results, you want to choose users who are already using the tool, in production.

Testing with Similar Users

In the games industry, it is very common that tool development begins before the content creators have joined the team, and that the deadline to deliver the tools is right before the users arrive and start producing assets. This often means that tools developers are scheduled to work on other tasks shortly after the users arrive and start using the tools for the first time. If the users have feedback about how the tools could be improved, there could be no one available to make changes. Oftentimes, nothing besides the most urgent problems with the base functionality of the tools are fixed. This often results in tools with an inferior user experience, which costs the game developer time and money in lost productivity over the course of production.

A better alternative would be to have the equivalent tools development resources working with the users but spread out all the way through production, instead of a big burst of work at the beginning. This will require that the people who manage tools developers understand the value of the User-Centered Design process, so that they can plan tools development tasks accordingly, which will require time and a cultural shift in the games industry. We will talk more about that in the final chapter.

In the meantime, if you find yourself in this situation, selecting other users who fit a similar profile may be your best option. If you are testing changes in code, and it is not possible to deploy the tool to the users' computers, do not let that stop you from getting feedback. Bring them to your desk, or to any computer that has an early version of the tool running. Alternatively, you can connect to a computer running the tool via remote desktop (as long as doing that does not significantly affect the user experience or measurements). The bottom line is that waiting for the perfect moment to test could result in a missed opportunity to improve the user experience. You should do everything that you can to ensure that the first time that the users lay eyes on the tool is not right before they start working with it for the first time.

How Many Users?

According to Jakob Nielsen, user testing with more than five users results in diminishing returns.[*] While there is some debate over this number, one thing is clear: if you limit your tests to five users, remember that those five users should have the same role and should do the same tasks. In other words, if you assign five users the task of using a level editor to place objects, but those users are a mix of animators, 3D artists, and programmers, you are unlikely to get accurate results. On the other hand, if you do this with five users who are all level designers responsible for placing objects in the level, you are much more likely to get accurate results.

Run the Test

Now it is time to get feedback. Meet with each user, show them the tool or pre-visualization, and go through your test plan one task at a time. As in the contextual analysis, resist the urge to help if they have difficulty understanding one of the tasks. Try to understand why they are having difficulty, and then move on to the next task. However, unlike the contextual analysis, you may choose to ask that the users do not talk out loud, since it could affect the time it takes them to complete a task. In this case, use your own judgment.

---

[*] You can read the article here: http://www.nngroup.com/articles/why-you-only-need-to-test-with-5-users/.

If you can, it is also recommended to perform the user tests with two people: one person assigning the tasks, and the other taking notes. When you are alone, it can be difficult to assign tasks, observe the user, and take notes all at once. Having a dedicated note-taker ensures that the person assigning the tasks can focus on the user and notice things that they might miss if they were taking notes.

Although user tests can take less time than a contextual analysis, try to keep them under an hour. Being the subject of a user test can be draining for some people. In any case, if the users are in production, they may not have more time than that. If you encounter resistance while running the user tests (either from the user you are testing or from their supervisor), ensure that everyone understands that the time required to run a user test is a small investment compared to the potential savings of time and money in the long term.

It can also be helpful to record a video of the user's screen, or their interaction with the pre-visualization. If an interesting or significant event occurs during the user test, make a note of the time that it occurs in the video, so that you can go back during the Analysis phase and grab a screenshot or short video clip.

WRAPPING UP

This chapter focused on the Evaluation phase of the User-Centered Design process. We learned how to evaluate a design and how to decide between pre-visualization and going straight to code. We also learned a series of techniques to be used during the Evaluation phase, such as sketching, paper prototyping, interactive prototyping, performing a heuristic evaluation, and finally, performing user tests.

In the next chapter, we will return to the Analysis phase, going back through the loop of the User-Centered Design process, and discuss the importance of comparing measurements.

CHAPTER 7

Back to Analysis

DÉJÀ VU

IF YOU HAVE BEEN READING UP UNTIL THIS POINT, you might be wondering why we are talking about the Analysis phase again. "We already did that in Chapter 4!"

The purpose of this chapter is to emphasize—once again—that the User-Centered Design process is an iterative cycle. Once you have completed the Evaluation phase, examine the feedback gathered during the Analysis phase to plan your next move.

Do We Have to Do Everything Over Again?

One of the misconceptions of the User-Centered Design process is that it is a heavy process and that each of the techniques must be used every time through the cycle. This is not true: while there is an up-front cost in doing Analysis for the first time, in subsequent iterations, the techniques are there to be used on an as-needed basis.

As you go through the loop, you may find that you missed an important task that the majority of users do on a regular basis. In this case, you can produce another task flow to add to the others. You may also discover important users of the tool that you were not aware of before. This could require doing more contextual analyses to discover their goals and mental models.

If not, you can spend the rest of the time focusing on analyzing the results of the Evaluation phase and preparing for the next round of adjustments in the Design phase.

COMPARING MEASUREMENTS

In game development, we are accustomed to gathering all sorts of measurements: the burn-down rate of a sprint, performance metrics of the CPU and GPU, how different types of memory are allocated, budgets for various types of expenses, the amount of information on each vertex of a mesh, and so on. Yet, when was the last time that the efficiency and learnability of the game development tools were measured on a regular basis?

One of the main reasons is due to the perception that it takes too much time to measure. However, consider this: if you go on a road trip, do you drive around aimlessly, hoping that you will soon arrive at your destination, or do you stop occasionally to check a map? Developing a tool without measuring is like driving around without occasionally checking a map (see Figure 7.1). While it is true that verifying measurements takes a little bit of time at each iteration, the goal is that the overall time will be lower, as opposed to barreling forward aimlessly in the hope that we are making the tool better.

Expert Opinions

If you have studied the history of computer science, you may have learned about Admiral Grace Hopper. She developed the first compiler, and she is credited with popularizing the term *debugging*. One of her most famous

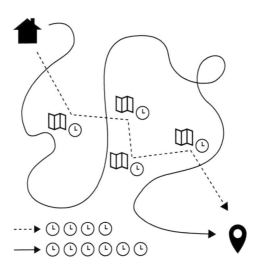

FIGURE 7.1 The importance of taking the time to analyze the results of the evaluation phase.

quotes is this: "One accurate measurement is worth more than a thousand expert opinions."

In the games industry, it is common to have an expert user or stakeholder whose job it is to represent the needs of all users with the same job description. When changes are made to a tool, we may ask this person to decide if the changes are good enough. In some cases, they may say that recent changes to the tool have made everyone more productive, and often the conversation ends there. However, how do we know that this is true? [*]

The Analysis phase is our opportunity to learn the answer to this question. By verifying and comparing the measurements, you can see if the changes have really helped to improve efficiency, learnability, or both. Each time you go through the Analysis phase, compare the measurements to the previous cycle, and keep a record for the next cycle. This is one of the most reliable ways to know if the changes made in the Design phase are moving the tool in the right direction.

It is important to note that this does not mean that we do not value the opinion of the expert users and stakeholders. On the contrary, by including them in the User-Centered Design process, they can use the information to make even better decisions, with less risk. This will help to build a stronger relationship between all of the people involved in the development of the tool, and keep everyone focused on improving the user experience.

---

[*] I was this person for several games, tools, and pipelines, and there is no doubt in my mind that my opinion was wrong on many occasions!

CHAPTER 8

Real-World User-Centered Design

INTRODUCTION

THE PURPOSE OF THIS CHAPTER is to present a "day in the life" account of a tools development team using the User-Centered Design process. This will give you a sense of what the process feels like, which can help you to understand how to implement it yourself.

The Cast
Stakeholders

- Sophie, project manager

- Ben, art director

Developers

- Daniel, tools programmer

- Francis, technical artist

The Company

This story takes place at a medium-sized game developer that has been in business for over ten years. They have developed their own engine and tools, which they have used to create games that have sold enough copies to keep them in business. However, very little effort has been put into improving the tools, due to perceived time and budget constraints. No one is measuring the performance of the users, and it is generally accepted that if the tool can create the content, it is "done."

As a result, some of the tools are not very easy to use and are frequently the source of frustration for the content creators. Most of the senior users who have been with the company for many years have given up on complaining and have simply accepted that the tools are the way they are.

The Situation

Sophie has recently been promoted to project manager. The last game that she shipped suffered from grueling overtime, productivity problems, lost data, and the slow ramp-up of new staff due to difficulty learning the tools. Some senior people quit shortly after the project, and the cost of retraining the new hires was significantly higher than if they had been able to keep their staff.

Sophie is currently in the production phase of her next project, and she is starting to see the same situation emerge from the last project, especially in the cut-scene pipeline. Concerned that history will repeat itself, and because work on cut-scenes will be starting soon, she decides that she wants to see if she should invest in improving the efficiency of the cut-scene pipeline.

She learns that two developers from another team, Daniel and Francis, have been using a new approach in their tools development work—the User-Centered Design process—and that they have been getting positive results. Although she wants to improve the tools, like a good project manager, she also wants to ensure that the benefits outweigh the costs.

Daniel and Francis have recently become available, so she asks them to join her team to focus on making the cut-scene pipeline more efficient. She requests that they keep her up to date on their sprint reports so she can track their progress.

THE PROCESS IN ACTION

Sprint 1

Analysis

Daniel and Francis start by interviewing the stakeholders. They know that Sophie's goal is to make the cut-scene pipeline more efficient. They also interview another stakeholder: Ben, the art director who is responsible for the cut-scenes. They learn that one of Ben's goals is to be able to request changes to the cameras and see the results so he can validate the composition. He also mentions that, during the last project he worked on, asking the animators to make changes to the camera took a very long time, which he found frustrating.

With these stakeholder goals in mind, Daniel and Francis move on to the next step: contextual analyses with the users who work on cut-scenes. In light of the art director's comments, they focus on the users who spend the most amount of time working with cameras, the animators. There are twelve animators in the cut-scene team, and they are scheduled to be working on cut-scenes for a total of six months.

During the contextual analyses, Daniel talks to the animators, while Francis takes notes. They begin by asking them what their goals are when working with the camera. Many of the goals that the users talk about can be linked to the producer and the art director: they want to adjust the camera, and they want to do it quickly. However, unlike the art director, their goal is not setting the composition of the camera but simply getting the job done so they can move on to their next task.

During the task of adjusting the camera, one of the actions is to adjust the depth of field. The depth of field has five values that the users can set: the start and end of the near blur, the start and end of the far blur, and the focus point distance. They mention that they sometimes get confused about what each value represents, that it is difficult to find the value they are looking for at a glance, and that they often have to readjust the values multiple times because they go beyond the minimum or maximum.

The junior users say that it is extremely difficult to use the depth of field tool. The senior users say that while it is not perfect, the junior users just have to adapt to it. In fact, the biggest complaint from the senior users is regarding something that is done only on occasion: copying the settings from one camera to another, which requires that they copy and paste the values one field at a time.

Some users even say that the depth of field tool does not need to be improved, mostly because it used to be worse! In the past, to change the depth of field, the users had to create a script file that contained commands to set the depth of field and attach that script file to the camera. This was a problem because many users would generate errors by forgetting to put a comma or a semicolon, misspelling the name of the command, and so on (see the left side of Figure 8.1).

To improve the situation, one of the tools programmers created a tool to set the depth of field: a window with a row of numeric boxes (see the right side of Figure 8.1). Even though some users feel that this tool is good

```
1  setdof(8, 32, 12, 42, 25);
2
3  setDOF(2, 26, 10, 18);
4
5  setDOF(4, 31, 11, 37, 22)
6
7  setDOF(5, 29, 14, 41 21);
8
9  setDOF(4, 30, 11, 39, 26);
```

Depth of Field	⊠
BLUR_BEGIN_FORE	8
BLUR_BEGIN_BACK	32
BLUR_END_FORE	12
BLUR_END_BACK	42
TARGET	25
Apply	

FIGURE 8.1   The previous (left) and current (right) methods for setting the depth of field of cameras.

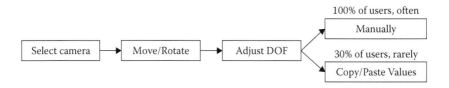

FIGURE 8.2   Task flow analysis for the process of setting up cameras for cut-scenes.

enough and that there is nothing left to do, it is clear to Daniel and Francis that this tool simply exposes the conceptual model of the depth of field script command, and that efficiency could be improved further.

Using the notes from their contextual analyses, Daniel and Francis start to build a task flow for adjusting the camera (see Figure 8.2).

After analyzing the results of the task flow, they observe that all of the users adjust the depth of field manually, and that they do it often. They decide that they will work on improving the efficiency of this action first, and that they will work on the copy/pasting of values from one camera to another later.

Design

To improve the efficiency of making manual adjustments using the depth of field tool, Daniel and Francis start by proposing a few small, iterative changes to the existing design.

To make the labels easier to scan, they apply the design technique of hierarchy. Next, to reduce the amount of time wasted by fixing invalid values, they replace the numeric boxes with sliders (following the Microsoft guidelines). This makes it clear that the values have a minimum and maximum. Finally, they modify the labels so that they are more familiar to the users. For example, the new term for "TARGET" is "Focus Distance," which matches the name of a similar value found in the depth of field camera settings of the animation tool that the animators are accustomed to using.

Evaluation

Daniel and Francis start to build their test plan. They make a list of tasks that can be used to measure the efficiency of manually adjusting the depth of field values. A few examples: "The art director would like you to increase the focus point of 'camera_2' by 10 units from frame 10 to frame 35 in the cut-scene 'Chapter1_ChaseB.' How would you do that?" and "You receive a bug report that the near blur of 'camera_3' is too high by 20 units throughout the cut-scene 'Chapter3_BossFightIntro.' How would you fix that?"

Because they are measuring efficiency, and Daniel is a programmer, they decide to go directly to code as opposed to pre-visualizing (Figure 8.3).

Before running the tests, Daniel and Francis also decide to perform a heuristic evaluation on the new version of the depth of field tool. A few of the heuristics jump out at them right away:

- Match between system and real world: The order and layout of the numeric boxes match the "setDOF" command more than the camera and the depth of field effect.

- Flexibility and efficiency of use: The users need to click on the "Apply" button every time they make a change.

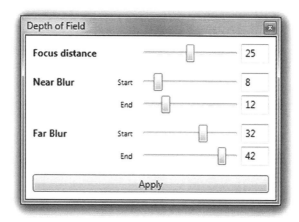

FIGURE 8.3   First iteration of the improved depth of field tool.

They deploy the changes and run their user tests. This time, Francis assigns tasks to the users while Daniel takes notes. They also record the users' screen while they are watching them work.

Sprint 2

Analysis

After the user tests are done, Daniel and Francis analyze the notes and the videos. They calculate that the users take an average of 20 seconds to complete all of the tasks from the user test. This will be their baseline measurement.

They also note that the majority of the users feel that the order of the sliders is confusing. Daniel and Francis believe that this is because they do not match the users' mental model of the camera, which is consistent with their findings during the heuristic evaluation. Daniel and Francis decide to do a brief contextual analysis focused on understanding the users' mental model of the camera.

After meeting with the users, they realize that many of them describe the camera from a side view, indicating the points at which the near and far blur occur. One of the users even does a sketch representing their mental model of the camera (see Figure 8.4). This inspires Daniel and Francis to improve the design.

Design

Francis has the idea to use the design technique of representation to lay out the sliders so that they match the users' mental model. The only issue is that Francis cannot find a multithumb slider in the Microsoft guidelines, so he looks to other content creation software. He finds examples of multithumb sliders in the Input Levels section of the Levels window in Adobe Photoshop (see the top of Figure 8.5), as well as with the Range

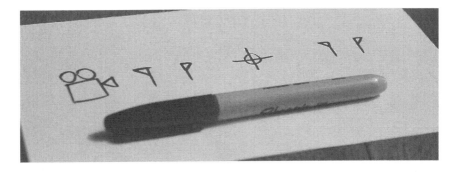

FIGURE 8.4   Exploring the mental model for depth of field.

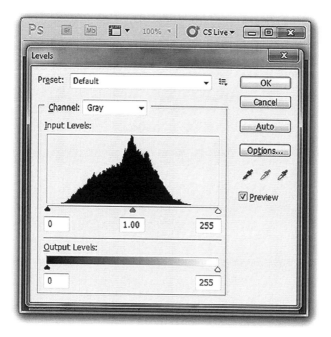

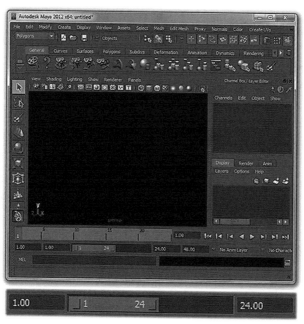

FIGURE 8.5 Researching common interaction patterns for a multi-thumb slider in Adobe Photoshop (top) and Autodesk Maya (bottom). Adobe product screenshot(s) reprinted with permission from Adobe Systems Incorporated. Autodesk screen shots reprinted with the permission of Autodesk, Inc.

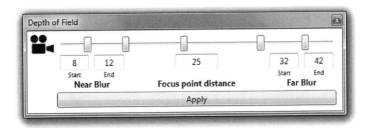

FIGURE 8.6   Second iteration of the improved depth of field tool.

slider in Autodesk Maya (see the bottom of Figure 8.5). He uses these as the interaction pattern.

Evaluation

Because this design contains controls that do not exist in their UI toolkit, and Daniel has an urgent bug to fix, Francis decides to pre-visualize. He creates a simple paper prototype and then performs a "Wizard of Oz" test.

The feedback from the users is positive. They say that the interface feels more natural than the previous tool, and they state that it will enable them to work faster. While this is good feedback, the paper prototype can only confirm that the new design matches the mental model, but it cannot determine if it increases efficiency. The only way to answer that will be to implement the changes. Once Daniel is available, they modify the interface and deploy the updated version (see Figure 8.6).

As they are modifying the interface, Daniel and Francis are approached by a few users who remind them that copying and pasting values is still a problem. Since they have made some progress on making manual adjustments, Daniel and Francis decide to see if they can improve copying and pasting values as well. They start by creating a user test for copying and pasting values from one camera to another, with tasks such as "Another animator set up 'cam_5' in the cut-scene 'Chapter5_IntroC,' and you want to use the same settings from frame 25. How would you do that?"

They run both the user test for manually adjusting values as well as the user test for copying and pasting values from one camera to another.

Sprint 3

Analysis

Daniel and Francis analyze the previous Evaluation phase and perform another measurement. They discover that the users now take an average of nine seconds to adjust the depth of field manually, which is an 11-second improvement from where they started. They also analyze the results from the copying and pasting camera values user test and arrive at a baseline measurement of seven seconds.

Design

To improve the efficiency even further, Daniel and Francis design two changes that use the technique of reducing excise.

First, they modify the tool so that the camera settings automatically update as soon as the sliders are modified. This allows the Apply button to be removed, so the users do not have to move their mouse down to the bottom of the tool and click every time they make a change.

Second, they add the ability to copy and paste from one camera to another. They expose this functionality to the users by implementing a standard Edit menu with copy and paste menu items. They associate the copy and paste commands to hotkeys that follow existing standards: Ctrl/Cmd+C and Ctrl/Cmd+V. This way, users can copy and paste values from one camera to another quickly and easily.

Evaluation

Since the changes are small, they decide to make them directly in code (see Figure 8.7). They run their user tests, and the results from the users are positive. All of the users appreciate that they are no longer required to click on the Apply button to update the depth of field in the viewport.

The users who copy and paste values are very happy that they can now do it faster. They also say that they think this will have the biggest impact on efficiency out of all the improvements that Daniel and Francis have made.

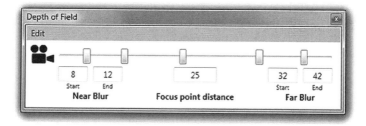

FIGURE 8.7   Third iteration of the improved depth of field tool.

Sprint 4

Analysis

Daniel and Francis examine the results and see that copying and pasting values has dropped from seven seconds to two seconds. That is an improvement of five seconds, which appears to be significant.

Removing the Apply button has made a big difference for all of the users of the tool, by lowering the time to adjust the depth of field manually to just three seconds. That is an overall improvement of 17 seconds.

CALCULATING THE RETURN ON INVESTMENT

Ben is very pleased with the improvements to the depth of field tool, and he tells Sophie about it. Although she trusts Ben's opinion, she wants to ensure that the time and money spent on improving the tools are paying off. She requests a status update from Daniel and Francis so that she can calculate the return on investment.* She uses the following information for her calculation:

- Cut-scene production will last six months (130 working days).

- Twelve users use the depth of field tool to adjust the camera. On average, they do this 90 times per 8-hour day.

- Four users copy and paste values between cameras. On average, they do this 10 times per 8-hour day.

- Each user working on the cut-scenes costs $10,000 per month.

This means that before Daniel and Francis made any improvements, all of the users together would spend over five man-months working with the depth of field over the six-month period, at a cost of almost $50,000 (see Figure 8.8).

After the improvements, the users are now spending a little under one man-month working with the depth of field over the six-month period, or around $7,500 (see Figure 8.9).

Although it may look like the improvements have resulted in a savings of $42,500, Sophie has to subtract the time spent by Daniel and Francis. Since they worked on the depth of field tool for three two-week sprints, and they cost $10,000 per man-month, the investment was $30,000. This

---

* You can find a variety of ROI calculators on the Human Factors website here: http://humanfactors. com/coolstuff/roi.asp.

Before Changes to Depth of Field Tool			
Duration (in days)	130	Cost/man-month	$10,000

Manually Change Values		Copy/Paste Values	
Number of users	12	Number of users	4
Seconds per action	20	Seconds per action	7
Times per day	90	Times per day	10
Total man-months	4.8	Total man-months	0.06
Total cost	$48,750	Total cost	$630

FIGURE 8.8   Calculating the cost of using the depth of field tool.

After Changes to Depth of Field Tool			
Duration (in days)	130	Cost/man-month	$10,000

Manually Change Values		Copy/Paste Values	
Number of users	12	Number of users	4
Seconds per action	3	Seconds per action	2
Times per day	90	Times per day	10
Total man-months	0.7	Total man-months	0.01
Total cost	$7,312	Total cost	$180

FIGURE 8.9   Calculating the cost of using the depth of field tool after the improvements to the user experience, in an effort to calculate the return on investment (ROI).

means that the total return on investment was $12,500. That is over a man-month of time that did not exist before the improvements, and Daniel and Francis are not done yet. In addition, it is important to note that any other production that uses the updated depth of field tool in the future will benefit from these improvements, immediately, at no cost.

Unfortunately, the copy and paste functionality did not result in as much of a return as was hoped, which emphasizes that the biggest impact comes from the improvements that affect the highest number of users, and those who use the tools the most frequently.

Ultimately, the improvements have had a positive return on investment. Sophie is satisfied with the results and asks Daniel and Francis to continue improving the user experience of the game development tools by applying the User-Centered Design process.

Conclusion

SUMMARY

The purpose of this book is to introduce you to concepts and techniques that can be used to improve the user experience of game development tools.

In Chapter 1, we learned the definition of a user experience, why we should improve the user experience, as well as the value of improving the user experience. We also learned the importance of balancing the needs of the various groups involved in the development of a tool.

Chapter 2 introduced you to the User-Centered Design process. We learned about the advantages of the process, as well as how to integrate it into Agile. We also discussed how to deal with a lack of time and resources.

Chapter 3 focused on what it means to be "User-Centered." In this chapter, we learned about the importance of focusing on the right users and ensuring that the features are useful for those users. We also discovered the power of pre-visualization and the differences between features and goals.

Chapter 4 presented the Analysis phase, where we discussed the importance of watching users work, an introduction to human–computer interaction, as well as the difference between a mental model and a conceptual model. We also learned about interviews, contextual analysis, and task flows, in addition to understanding how to measure improvements to the user experience.

Chapter 5 was all about the Design phase: how the brain and the eyes work together, as well as visual language and interaction patterns. We also learned a wide variety of techniques that can be used to address common design problems, as well as common interaction patterns for each.

In Chapter 6, we discovered how to choose the right strategy for evaluating our designs. We also learned pre-visualization techniques and heuristic evaluation. Finally, we learned how to build and run user tests.

Chapter 7 brought us back to the Analysis phase to compare our measurements and to prepare for another cycle through the User-Centered Design process.

Finally, Chapter 8 walked us through a day in the life of a tools development team tasked with improving the user experience of a tool, to give us a better sense of how it feels to apply the User-Centered Design process.

CLOSING WORD

Culture Shift

Throughout this book, we have used examples from Apple. This is not because every single one of their products has the best user experience—they certainly have made some mistakes over the years—but their products provide good examples that can be used to support the concepts and techniques presented in this book. However, you might be wondering, what is their secret? How do they do it?

One of the misconceptions about why Apple products are so successful is that they have the best designers in the world. While their designers are certainly very good, that is not the only factor at play.

An interview with former Apple senior designer Mark Kawano sheds some light on the truth: everyone at Apple works together to improve the user experience. "It's actually the engineering culture, and the way the organization is structured to appreciate and support design. Everybody there is thinking about UX and design, not just the designers. And that's what makes everything about the product so much better ... much more than any individual designer or design team."*

The games industry needs to make the user experience of tools a priority. To do that, we need the User-Centered Design process to become as common as using Scrum, profiling GPU performance, and creating cutscene storyboards. When that happens, we will start to see the culture shift necessary to make big improvements.

Where to Begin?

Now that you have read this book, the first step is to start applying the User-Centered Design process to your own tools development work. Once you feel confident with the process and you have had success that you can measure, the next step is to spread the word. Help people understand

---

* You can read the full interview here: http://www.fastcodesign.com/3030923/4-myths-about-apple-design-from-an-ex-apple-designer.

how User-Centered Design can be integrated into the tools development pipeline at your studio, because every studio is different. Tell your colleagues how you achieved your successes, and what you learned from your failures. Everyone in the games industry should be aware of the incredible potential that is waiting to be unlocked by improving the user experience of our game development tools.

There is no right or wrong time to start. Start small, and then work your way up. Do a heuristic evaluation of that tool you have been working on. Set up a few interviews with the stakeholders and contextual analyses with the users so you can establish and track measurements. Apply one of the many techniques found in the Design chapter.

Improving the user experience is an iterative process, which means you can begin at any time ... and that time might as well be now!

Are you ready? Three ... two ... one ... go!

Thanks

This book was written, illustrated, and edited in airplanes, trains, hotel rooms, and cafes, in four cities, on two continents, on one laptop. It would not have been possible without the following people.

Jim Brown, Liam Grieg, Tom Hoferek, Corey Johnson, Thérèse Migan, Jason Parks, and Karine Thériault for their invaluable feedback. Dominique Roussy, for giving me my first job in the games industry. My first computer science teacher, Susan Van Gelder, for seeing my interest in the fusion of programming and art, and providing me with the tools I needed. Mike Acton, for his contributions to game tools usability, and for providing the foreword. Geoff Evans, Jeff Ward, Dan Goodman, and all other past, present, and future members of the Toolsmiths IGDA SIG, for working to bring the challenges of game tools development into the spotlight. Ubisoft, for giving me the opportunity to turn my passion for user experience and content creation tools into a career. Pierre-Luc Tremblay, for introducing me to *The Inmates Are Running the Asylum*—and to Alan Cooper for writing it. Rick Adams, Maura Cregan, Marsha Pronin, Amy Blalock, Charlotte Byrnes, and everyone at CRC Press who helped to make this book possible. Lucy Suchman, Jason Mitchell, and Sara Lott at the Computer History Museum for providing a few of the images in this book. Sony, for making a tough little laptop that accompanied me throughout this long journey. My big brother and big sister, who prepared me for the real world by sandwiching me in the back seat of our parents' car. My wife and children for reminding me that there is more to life than just content creation tools ... which I believe, most of the time. Thank you, Andrea, Benjamin, and Sophie ... I love you!

Works Cited & Recommended Reading

Adlin, Tamara, and John Pruitt. *The Essential Persona Lifecycle: Your Guide to Building and Using Personas.* San Francisco, CA: Morgan Kaufmann, 2010.

Alexander, Christopher, Sara Ishikawa, and Murray Silverstein. *A Pattern Language: Towns, Buildings, Construction.* New York: Oxford University Press, 1977.

Anderson, Jonathan, John McRee, Robb Wilson, et al. *Effective UI.* Beijing: O'Reilly, 2010.

Buxton, William. *Sketching User Experiences: Getting the Design Right and the Right Design.* Amsterdam: Elsevier/Morgan Kaufmann, 2007.

Cooper, Alan. *The Inmates Are Running the Asylum.* Indianapolis, IN: Sams, 1999.

Cooper, Alan, Robert Reimann, and Dave Cronin. *About Face 3: The Essentials of Interaction Design.* 3rd ed. Indianapolis, IN: Wiley Pub., 2007.

Gamma, Erich, Richard Helm, Ralph Johnson, and John Vlissides. *Design Patterns: Elements of Reusable Object-Oriented Software.* Upper Saddle River, NJ: Addison-Wesley, 1995.

Gladwell, Malcolm. *David and Goliath: Underdogs, Misfits, and the Art of Battling Giants.* New York: Little Brown & Company, 2013.

Gothelf, Jeff, and Josh Seiden. *Lean UX: Applying Lean Principles to Improve User Experience.* Sebastopol, CA: O'Reilly Media, 2013.

Hawkins, Jeff, and Sandra Blakeslee. *On Intelligence.* New York: Times Books, 2004.

Hiltzik, Michael A. *Dealers of Lightning: Xerox PARC and the Dawn of the Computer Age.* New York: HarperBusiness, 1999.

Johnson, Jeff. *Designing with the Mind in Mind: Simple Guide to Understanding User Interface Design Rules.* Amsterdam: Morgan Kaufmann Publishers/Elsevier, 2010.

Krug, Steve. *Don't Make Me Think!: A Common Sense Approach to Web Usability.* 2nd ed. Berkeley, CA: New Riders Pub., 2006.

McConnell, Steve. *Code Complete: A Practical Handbook of Software Construction.* 2nd ed. Redmond, WA: Microsoft Press, 2004.

Myers, Brad A. "The Importance of Percent-Done Progress Indicators for Computer–Human Interfaces." *ACM SIGCHI Bulletin* 16, no. 4 (1985): 11–17.

Nielsen, Jakob. "First Rule of Usability? Don't Listen to Users." Nielsen Norman Group. http://www.nngroup.com/articles/first-rule-of-usability-dont-listen-to-users/ (accessed July 15, 2014).

Nielsen, Jakob. "Why You Only Need to Test with 5 Users." Nielsen Norman Group. http://www.nngroup.com/articles/why-you-only-need-to-test-with-5-users (accessed July 15, 2014).

Nielsen, Jakob. "Response Time Limits." Nielsen Norman Group. http://www.nngroup.com/articles/response-times-3-important-limits/ (accessed July 15, 2014).

Nielsen, Jakob. *Usability Engineering*. Boston: Academic Press, 1993.

Norman, Donald A. *The Design of Everyday Things*. New York: Basic Books, 1988.

Portigal, Steve. *Interviewing Users: How to Uncover Compelling Insights*. Brooklyn, NY: Rosenfeld Media, 2013.

Saffer, Dan. *Designing for Interaction: Creating Innovative Applications and Devices*. 2nd ed. Berkeley, CA: New Riders, 2010.

Sanders, Elizabeth B.-N. "Converging Perspectives: Product Development Research for the 1990s." *Design Management Journal* (Former Series) 3, no. 4 (1992): 49–54.

Suchman, Lucille Alice. *Human–Machine Reconfigurations: Plans and Situated Actions*. 2nd ed. Cambridge: Cambridge University Press, 2007.

Sy, Desiree. "Adapting Usability Investigations for Agile User-Centered Design." *Journal of Usability Studies* 2, no. 3 (May 2007), 112–132. (Available at http://uxpajournal.org/wp-content/uploads/pdf/agile-ucd.pdf.)

Vlaskovits, Patrick. "Henry Ford, Innovation, and That 'Faster Horse' Quote." *Harvard Business Review*. http://blogs.hbr.org/2011/08/henry-ford-never-said-the-fast/ (accessed July 15, 2014).

Weinschenk, Susan. *100 Things Every Designer Needs to Know about People*. Berkeley, CA: New Riders, 2011.

Wilson, Mark. "4 Myths about Apple Design, from an Ex-Apple Designer." Co. Design. http://www.fastcodesign.com/3030923/4-myths-about-apple-design-from-an-ex-apple-designer (accessed July 15, 2014).

TOOLS & GUIDELINES

Microsoft Windows User Experience Guidelines: http://msdn.microsoft.com/library/windows/desktop/dn688964.aspx

Apple OSX User Experience Guidelines: https://developer.apple.com/library/mac/documentation/UserExperience/Conceptual/AppleHIGuidelines/Intro/Intro.html

W3C standards for contrast: http://www.w3.org/TR/UNDERSTANDING-WCAG20/visual-audio-contrast-contrast.html

Human Factors International ROI Calculators: http://humanfactors.com/coolstuff/roi.asp

Measuring Usability article on the SUS (System Usability Scale): http://www.measuringusability.com/sus.php

Jakob Nielsen's 10 Usability Heuristics: http://www.nngroup.com/articles/ten-usability-heuristics/

Trademarks

Adobe®, the Adobe® logo, Adobe® Audition®, Adobe® Photoshop®, Adobe® Premiere Pro®, and Adobe® Illustrator® are either registered trademarks or trademarks of Adobe Systems Incorporated in the United States and/or other countries.

Autodesk®, the Autodesk® logo, Autodesk® Maya®, Autodesk® Combustion®, and Autodesk® 3ds max® are registered trademarks or trademarks of Autodesk, Inc., and/or its subsidiaries and/or affiliates in the United States and/or other countries.

The Unity® name, logo, brand, and other trademarks or images featured or referred to within this book are licensed from and are the sole property of Unity Technologies. Neither this book, its author, nor the publisher is affiliated with, endorsed by, or sponsored by Unity Technologies or any of its affiliates.

Microsoft®, the Microsoft® logo, Office®, Word®, Excel®, PowerPoint®, Visual Studio®, Halo®, Expression Blend®, and Windows® are either registered trademarks or trademarks of Microsoft Corporation in the United States and/or other countries.

Apple®, the Apple® logo, GarageBand®, Mac®, Xcode®, iTunes®, iPhone®, iPod®, iOS®, and OSX® are trademarks of Apple, Inc., registered in the United States and other countries.

NVIDIA®, the NVIDIA® logo, NVIDIA® Texture Tools, and the NVIDIA® Normal Map filter are trademarks and/or registered trademarks of NVIDIA Corporation in the United States and other countries.

Audacity® software is copyright (c) 1999-2014 Audacity Team. The name Audacity® is a registered trademark of Dominic Mazzoni.

Balsamiq® is a registered trademark of Giacomo Guilizzoni, licensed to Balsamiq SRL and Balsamiq Studios, LLC, used with permission.

StarCraft® and Blizzard Entertainment® are trademarks or registered trademarks of Blizzard Entertainment, Inc., in the United States and/or other countries.

Qt is a registered trademark of Digia Plc and/or its subsidiaries.

Xerox®, the Xerox® logo, and the Xerox® 8200 are registered trademarks of Xerox Corporation in the United States and/or other countries.

iRiver, the iRiver logo, and the iRiver H300 are registered trademarks of iRiver Limited in the Republic of Korea and/or other countries.

Epic, Epic Games, and the Epic Games logo are trademarks or registered trademarks of Epic Games, Inc., in the United States and elsewhere.

Amazon, Kindle, Storyteller, and Mechanical Turk are trademarks of Amazon.com, Inc., or its affiliates.

Sony, the Sony logo, PlayStation, Vaio, Emotion Engine, and Cell Broadband Engine are trademarks or registered trademarks of Sony Computer Entertainment, Inc., in the United States, other countries, or both and is used under license therefrom.

Pixar is a registered trademark of Pixar Animation Studios.

Logitech is a registered trademark of Logitech International in the United States and other countries.

Valve, the Valve logo, and Team Fortress 2 are trademarks and/or registered trademarks of Valve Corporation.

Mad Catz and the Mad Catz logo are trademarks or registered trademarks of Mad Catz Interactive, Inc., its subsidiaries and affiliates.

"Minicons Free Vector Icons Pack" by Webalys (http://www.webalys.com/minicons) used under CC BY 3.0 license (http://creativecommons.org/licenses/by/3.0/).

Index

Printed and bound by CPI Group (UK) Ltd, Croydon, CR0 4YY

22/10/2024

01777624-0020